"For each of his stories, Ian identifies a key precept from the *Art of War* that encapsulates the strategy employed by a particular prince to secure the throne. Paradoxically, a central principle of Sun Tzu's teachings is the avoidance of violence.

Many of us engaged in studying China past and present aspire to reach out to a wider audience, to make what we know accessible beyond a narrow circle of academic specialists. With this book, Ian has succeeded brilliantly in doing exactly that, in a way that is useful to a wide readership. The stories presented here are gripping; the book is a great read."

Professor Robert Chard
Associate Professor of Classical Chinese
Oxford University

"Ian Huen's first book comes at important point in China's relations with the rest of the world. As it reemerges as one of the world's largest economies and major powers, it is more important than ever before to better understand China's dynamics and processes. There is no better way to do this than through its history and how its history reflects in personal and business dynamics. This book provides an invaluable contribution, as it masterfully applies elements of China's historical and cultural foundations to draw lessons for business and strategy."

Professor Douglas Arner,
Kerry Holdings Professor in Law
University of Hong Kong

"Ian Huen's *The Rising Sons* is an incisive romp through the most fraught imperial successions in Chinese history. Drawing on the wisdom of Sun Tzu, Huen traces how heirs who successfully ascended to the throne hunted like leopards, biding their time in hiding, maximizing their likelihood of success while maintaining their cover, and then striking swiftly when the opportunity presented itself. The imperial Chinese court was an uncertain, fractious, and often violent political environment. Yet however well they played the game of thrones, the successful heirs, as Huen points out, were not always wise or effective at governing once in power. Huen's trenchant analysis has lessons for the perils of succession and governance today."

Professor Justin Hastings
Professor in International Relations and Comparative Politics
University of Sydney

"Through our numerous discussions, especially during his guest lectures in my program, Ian had always been able to apply Chinese history to modern international business settings that proved to be edifying for his audience. He has done precisely that in *The Rising Sons* as well. Bravo! I am certain this book will be as beneficial for all its readers as Ian's lectures had been for my EMBA students."

Professor Andrew Chan
Emeritus Professor (Department of Marketing)
Director of the Executive MBA Program (2002–2020)
The Chinese University of Hong Kong

THE
RISING
SONS

**China's Imperial Succession
& The Art of War**

THE RISING SONS

China's Imperial Succession & The Art of War

Ian Huen

Aptorum Group

World Scientific

NEW JERSEY · LONDON · SINGAPORE · BEIJING · SHANGHAI · HONG KONG · TAIPEI · CHENNAI · TOKYO

Published by

World Scientific Publishing Co. Pte. Ltd.

5 Toh Tuck Link, Singapore 596224

USA office: 27 Warren Street, Suite 401-402, Hackensack, NJ 07601

UK office: 57 Shelton Street, Covent Garden, London WC2H 9HE

Library of Congress Cataloging-in-Publication Data

Names: Huen, Ian, author.

Title: The rising sons : China's imperial succession & The art of war / by Ian Huen.

Description: New Jersey : World Scientific, [2022] | Includes bibliographical references and index.

Identifiers: LCCN 2021029594 | ISBN 9789811240638 (hardcover) |
    ISBN 9789811240645 (ebook for institutions) | ISBN 9789811240652 (ebook for individuals)

Subjects: LCSH: Sunzi, active 6th century B.C. Sunzi bing fa. | Emperors--Succession--China. |
    Strategy. | China--Kings and rulers--Biography. | China--Politics and government. |
    China--History.

Classification: LCC DS740.2 .H839 2022 | DDC 355.02--dc23

LC record available at https://lccn.loc.gov/2021029594

British Library Cataloguing-in-Publication Data

A catalogue record for this book is available from the British Library.

For any available supplementary material, please visit
https://www.worldscientific.com/worldscibooks/10.1142/12379#t=suppl

Desk Editor: Nicole Ong

Typeset by Stallion Press
Email: enquiries@stallionpress.com

About the Author

Ian Huen is the founder and Chief Executive Officer of Aptorum Group (Nasdaq: APM), a global pharmaceutical company dedicated to developing and commercialising therapeutic and diagnostics technologies to tackle unmet medical needs. He is a part-time lecturer for Technology, Innovation and Entrepreneurship at the Master of Science in Business Management programme offered by the Shenzhen Finance Institute at the Chinese University of Hong Kong (Shenzhen campus). He graduated from Princeton University with an A.B. degree in Economics. He also holds a Master of Arts degree in the Comparative and Public History Program at the Chinese University of Hong Kong and is the awardee of the Scholarship for Outstanding History MA Student for 2015–2016.

His passion for Chinese history and culture has led him to become an enthusiastic proponent of integrating modern global business with traditional Chinese wisdom. He has delivered numerous lectures at forums such as the Institute of China Studies and the EMBA programme at the Chinese University of Hong Kong, on topics such as the management principles of Cao Cao to the poetic world of the Song dynasty literalist Su Dong Po.

Preface

It gives me great pleasure to offer a few words of introduction to this highly entertaining and informative book, by a remarkable author I have known for many years.

China's rich history is a blank to many people in the Euro-American world. Most are generally aware that China is a big country, and that it has been around a long time. Many are less aware of China's prominent place in world history, that it represents an entire civilization equivalent to the Roman Empire in antiquity, and later the whole of Europe. After the fall of the Roman Empire the size of the Chinese economy was often much larger than that of Europe, and it was only with the Industrial Revolution that the western end of Eurasia surged decisively ahead. Against the background of world history, the recent rise of East Asia is not a rise at all, but rather the return of a long-term equal balance.

Over such a span of time in such a large geographical area, it is hardly surprising that a lot was going on. We are fortunate that China is a literate civilization, with a textual history going back more than 3000 years, so we do know a fair bit about its history. One estimate of China's literary output is that more than half the world's books before the year 1500 were produced there, in part because paper and printing were invented centuries before they reached Europe. This means we have access to a wealth of records from which historians in China and beyond have constructed many narratives of China's past.

The current volume offers a new narrative different from any other I know of, a book that reaches parts of the detail of Chinese history that others do not, and does so in a way that is accessible and entertaining. This is attributable to Ian Huen's unique viewpoint, that of a highly successful businessman with all the wide real-world experience that brings, combined with a lifelong passion for Chinese history and a hands-on familiarity with the rich documentary record that allows him to bring it to life. Here he presents a series of stories covering more than 2,000 years from the third century BC to the nineteenth century AD, stories of struggles for succession at the centre of power, telling how different imperial princes manoeuvred from unlikely positions to become sovereigns of the entire empire. These come direct from the primary source documents — despite the dramatic nature of these narratives, there is no fiction here. Each story is set in context with concise explanations of the historical context needed to understand them, as valuable and informative as the stories themselves.

A central theme in all these stories is strategy. To understand China, one must understand how Chinese strategy works. Strategy of all sorts, especially political and military, was a field of considerable practical, and theoretical, sophistication in China from the fourth and third centuries BC. One example of this best known in the west is the *Art of War* attributed to Sun Tzu, a much-translated text enunciating strategic principles extending beyond warfare, principles modern people in business still find useful as a source of inspiration.

For each of his stories, Ian identifies a key precept from the *Art of War* that encapsulates the strategy employed by a particular prince to secure the throne. Paradoxically, a central principle of Sun Tzu's teachings is the avoidance of violence. The highest form of military victory is one achieved without battle. In keeping with this, the princes in these stories rarely resort to violence. Rather, they rely on strategic positioning, avoiding the limelight, misdirection, knowing when to remain inactive and when to strike, and how to read and exploit human psychology.

Many of us engaged in studying China past and present aspire to reach out to a wider audience, to make what we know accessible beyond a narrow circle of academic specialists. With this book, Ian has succeeded brilliantly in doing exactly that, in a way that is useful to a wide readership. The stories presented here are gripping; the book is a great read.

Robert L. Chard
Associate Professor of Classical Chinese,
Tutorial Fellow in Chinese;
China Centre, St Anne's College;
University of Oxford.

Contents

"Water shapes its course according to the nature of the ground over which it flows; the soldier works out his victory in relation to the foe whom he is facing."
The Art of War, Chapter 6
《水因地而制流，兵因敌而制胜。》
孙子兵法第六章

"In military combat, what is most difficult is turning the circuitous into the straight and adversity into advantage."
The Art of War, Chapter 7
《军争之难者，以迂为直，以患为利。》
孙子兵法第七章

"Attaining one hundred victories in one hundred battles is not the pinnacle of excellence. Subjugating the enemy's army without fighting is."
The Art of War, Chapter 3
《是故百战百胜，非善之善者也；不战而屈人之兵，善之善者也。》
孙子兵法第三章

"It is the nature of the army to stress speed; to take advantage of the enemy's absence; to travel unanticipated roads; and to attack when they are not alert."
The Art of War, Chapter 11
《兵之情主速，乘人之不及，由不虞之道，攻其所不戒也。》
孙子兵法第十一章

"Deception is the essence of human engagement. The competent must show incompetence overtly and the ambitious must demonstrably express his lack of ambition."
The Art of War, Chapter 1
《兵者，诡道也。故能而示之不能，用而示之不用。》
孙子兵法第一章

"Military operations must always be kept short so the winner prepares himself as if he was in constant danger and his execution must be swift. His preparation is like a drawn bow and his execution is similar to that of releasing the arrow."
The Art of War, Chapter 5
《故善战者，其势险，其节短。势如扩弩，节如发机。》
孙子兵法第五章

"The leader uses mercy to gather support and then commands his supporters with discipline."
The Art of War, Chapter 9
《故令之以文，齐之以武。》
孙子兵法第九章

Introduction

The Art of War (孙子兵法) is more like a great heritage site or tourist attraction than a book. People do not just read it. They return to it again and again. When they are bullied in the office or want to get a promotion or salary raise; when they feel they are being manipulated in a relationship or losing control in a situation; or when they are puzzled by what is happening in the world. Sun Tzu's (孙子) classic is perpetually useful because it is as much a user guide on how to conduct oneself and deal with others as a work of philosophy and tactics. It will continue to inspire and illuminate as long as politics remains a powerful presence in our daily lives.

Leadership succession in Imperial China is a fascinating but relatively under-studied subject, where the political becomes intensely personal and vice versa. The purpose of this book is to bring the wisdom of Sun Tzu to understand this field of human conflict that had shaped the course of Chinese history. By closely examining how the subtle application of *The Art of War* strategies made the difference between winning and losing in a complex struggle of life and death, where one false move by the players could also be their last, one gains insight into why Sun Tzu's classic, written over 2,500 years ago, is still useful to our lives in big and small ways. To this end, I opt for a broader interpretation of the classic with an emphasis on its relevance to the everyday life and practical uses for the common people.

The heroes featured in this book belonged to the rare breed of people Sun Tzu calls "善战者" (*shan zhan zhe*), which literally means "the good fighter". But to understand them as people "who excel in warfare" is to sell Sun Tzu short. Combat in life can take many forms and no one understands this better than Sun Tzu. Most of the battles, he knows, cannot be won by just flexing one's muscle and using brute force. The true winner, which is what the term "善战者" really means, wins by avoiding overt aggression. He bides his time to build up strategic advantages and waits for the enemy to expose his vulnerability. When he is confident of victory, he strikes decisively.

As we will soon find out, this is exactly what one needs to do to come out on top in the fierce and deadly battle for imperial succession. An in-depth analysis of the "Game of Thrones" in Imperial China through the lens of Sun Tzu lays bare the inner workings of the imperial court and the power dynamics governing the convoluted inter-relationships among the emperor and his consorts and children, his ministers and generals as well as the in-laws. It also dispels the notion that "the good fighters" and "those who excel in warfare" must prove themselves on the battlefield, like Achilles and Leonidas I of ancient Greece. What they excelled in, especially for the successful crown princes — the rising sons of the title — was concealing, not revealing, their ambitions. As the Chinese saying goes, a wise man would not stand near a collapsing wall.

By camouflaging their imperial desires, the rising sons were able to survive through political turmoil. But concealing one's ambition is not the same as lapsing into passivity. They achieved succession success by being empathetic with the ones who made the final decision: their father emperors. Contrary to conventional wisdom, the aging emperor did not want from his sons mesmerizing talent which he might even find threatening. What he wanted instead was love and care. In this aspect, he was just like every father, only more. The clever son knew the way to becoming his father's choice was through his heart. His demonstration of filial piety, therefore, was in fact the swift military action espoused by Sun Tzu. The nine historical figures we examine in this book all followed the master's process of winning through secrecy of intention, maximizing the probability of success, and taking swift action to secure final victory. What they practiced was no less than *The Art of War* in Chinese imperial succession.

Ying Yiren

King of Qin

Insignificant Consort

Crown Prince of Qin

Lady Huayang

Adopts

Zhao Ji

YING YIREN

First Emperor Of China

Chapter 1

Ying Yiren's Path of Least Resistance to Power

Dynasty: Qin (秦)

Period: circa 250 BC to 230 BC

Key Players:

Qin Zhuangxiang Wang Ying Yiren (秦庄襄王嬴异人)**:** The hostage prince, later crown prince, then King of Qin with the title Qin Zhuangxiang Wang (秦庄襄王)

Lady Huayang (华阳夫人)**:** Favorite Consort of the Crown Prince of Qin, later Ying Yiren's adoptive mother

Zhao Ji (赵姬)**:** Concubine first to the merchant, later to Ying Yiren, mother of the First Emperor of China (秦始皇)

Qin Shihuang Ying Zheng (秦始皇嬴政)**:** Son of Ying Yiren and Zhao Ji, better known as the First Emperor of China or Qin Shihuang (秦始皇)

Lü Buwei (吕不韦)**:** Originally a merchant, assisted Ying Yiren rise to the Qin throne, killed by the First Emperor of China

> *"Water shapes its course according to the nature of the ground over which it flows; the soldier works out his victory in relation to the foe whom he is facing."*

The Art of War, Chapter 6

《水因地而制流，兵因敌而制胜。》

孙子兵法第六章

HISTORICAL CONTEXT

The Qin Empire was the first regime that unified China under one emperor.[1] The Qin state, its regional predecessor, was famous for its fierce fighting force which its enemies referred to as "The Army of Wolves and Tigers".[2] The thousands of life-sized clay models of soldiers, horses, and chariots around the grand

---

[1] Prior to the Zhou Dynasty (周朝) which was established in 1046 BC, the previous dynasties Xia (夏) and Shang (商) were tribal regimes and their histories spotty. The Zhou regime followed the feudal system where the Zhou King granted his relatives and key collaborators of his kingdom lordship over the lands in what is now northern China along the Yellow River (黄河). Even though these were independent jurisdictions, they remained subordinated to the Zhou King, until around 770 BC when the central government began to lose its prestige and military might. China entered into a tumultuous era which was roughly split between the Spring and Autumn Period (春秋时代) from 770 to 476 BC and the Warring States Period (战国时代) from 476 to 221 BC. China was united under the leadership of the First Emperor Qin Shihuang (秦始皇) and the empire was named after his original kingdom Qin (秦). It was the first time in Chinese history where this large land mass in East Asia was governed by a centralized government with a functioning bureaucracy rather than a regime comprised of semi-independent vassal states.

[2] The real rise of the Qin happened during the early part of the Warring States Period in the 350s BC under the reforms of the great minister Shang Yang (商鞅). Shang Yang's reforms mainly comprised of focusing the vassal state's resources on agriculture and war; with the former's purpose being to provide for the latter. Shang created strong incentive structures for fighting courageously in the battlefield. For example, up to this present day, the Chinese word for the head is "*shouji*" (首级) which directly translates to "head" "rank". The source came from Shang Yang's reform: Qin citizens were divided by rank and one of the ways to get ahead is to come back from battle with "heads" of the enemy soldiers. A head counted for a rise in rank and therefore the character is included in the Chinese term. Such incentive schemes created a fierce Qin army as the other warring states came to fear them and referred to them as "The Army of Wolves and Tigers" (狼虎之师).

mausoleum of the First Emperor give a glimpse of this incredible fighting machine. However, while the First Emperor is perhaps the most written about ruler of ancient China, his father Ying Yiren remains an elusive and shadowy presence in Chinese history.

THE MERCHANT AND THE PRINCE

Ying Yiren was a grandson of the King of Qin. He was the middle child of the then Crown Prince of the Qin state[3] and one of his twenty sons. His improbable ascendance to the throne was partly owed to a successful but lowly merchant, Lü Buwei.

The merchant was ambitious, as demonstrated by the following exchange he had with his father:

Lü Buwei inquired, "What is the rate of return on capital for farming?"

Lü Buwei's father replied, "Ten times."

Lü Buwei then asked, "How about the return on capital for trading?"

Lü Buwei's father said, "A hundred times."

Lü Buwei further probed, "How about the return on capital for helping a person to inherit the throne and lord over all the lands under heaven?

Lü Buwei's father warned, "Infinity! However, be careful lest you perish while trying."

Undeterred, Lü Buwei proceeded with his plan to enter into politics. His midlife career change was motivated by more than the prospect of greater profitability. The social status of a businessman was extremely low in ancient China. They led precarious lives too. They would see their fortunes evaporate and wealth confiscated whenever the political winds blew the wrong way for them.

Lü Buwei set his eyes on Ying Yiren who was staying in the capital of Qin's enemy state[4] as a de facto hostage. The enemy state, with a dominant military

---

[3]Ying Yiren's father was the Crown Prince of Qin with the title *An Guojun* (安国君).

[4]Ying Yiren was acting as a hostage in Handan (邯郸), the capital city of the state of Zhao (赵国). To make matters worse for Ying Yiren, Qin was in constant war with Zhao as the latter was the main military force in the middle of China at the time. It was during Ying Yiren's stay in Zhao when the Battle of Changping (长平之战) happened in 260 BC. The Zhao general Zhao Kuo (赵括) was said to possess an amazing amount of military theoretical knowledge but scarcely any real experience. His army was annihilated by a much

force, had been at constant war with Qin. Sending one of its many princes to stay in the enemy state was a low-cost move to establish goodwill and lower the guard of the enemy. It also made clear how disposable Ying Yiren was to the Qin state.

Ying Yiren's low status, however, was exactly what drew Lü Buwei to him. No matter what his father the Crown Prince or his grandfather the Qin King saw in him, Ying Yiren had royal blood. The fact that he was sidelined in a major way only implied a potential value investment.

Lü Buwei set up a meeting with Ying Yiren and said to him, "I can make your household great!"

Ying Yiren, without much enthusiasm, replied, "Why don't you make your own household great and then proceed to make mine great?", displaying the typical scorn ancient aristocrats and scholars had for the merchant class.[5]

Lü Buwei, not one to be insulted easily, said, "I'll make your household great so you could make mine great."

He then provided Ying Yiren with a proposal: Ying Yiren had little clout in the Qin court because he was his father the Crown Prince's middle child and just one of the twenty sons he had. That his mother was not anywhere close to being the Crown Prince's favorite consort did not help. However, Lü Buwei told Ying Yiren, there was still a way out. Ying Yiren's father had a favorite consort named Lady Huayang. Despite her husband's fondness for her, Lady Huayang did not have any sons. This boded ill for her future as her status would deteriorate rapidly after the death of her husband. A son would guarantee her long-term well-being.

Ying Yiren's royal blood and lack of status, the merchant explained to him, would complement Lady Huayang's "high status and lack of a son" perfectly. Ying Yiren was too shrewd a calculator himself not to concur. In fact, there was very little that he could lose in allowing the merchant to fight for the title of heir to his father, the Crown Prince, for him. By accepting his offer, Ying Yiren was able to maximize the potential return of becoming the ruler of Qin by risking very little.

---

shrewder Qin general Bai Qi (白起), with Bai Qi burying four hundred thousand Zhao prisoners of war alive to eliminate any potential comeback for the losing state. The popular idiom "discussing war on paper" (纸上谈兵), referring to Zhao Kuo's defeat, is used in the Chinese language to describe anyone who talks the talk but cannot walk the walk.

[5] The contempt for businesspeople was so great that, for example in the Western Jin (西晋) Dynasty (265–330 AD), businessmen had to wear a black shoe on one foot and white in the other to show their trade required being both good and evil, implying they could not be trusted.

Having received Ying Yiren's blessing, Lü Buwei went to meet Lady Huayang's brother and said to him, "You are treated with such high esteem because your sister is the Crown Prince's favorite. Yet according to the dictates of nature, if one serves her master with her beauty, love will fade when her beauty fades. Your sister does not have a son and one day when she becomes old, she will fall out of favor with the Crown Prince. Even if she will not, when the old Crown Prince dies, another woman's son will become the King of Qin and she will lose her status. That is where the son of the Crown Prince, Ying Yiren, comes in. He is now in the enemy state and is ready to be adopted by your sister. Please convince your sister to meet with me and I will explain the situation to her."

He then met with Lady Huayang's sister and gave her a similar account of events. Shaken and worried, the brother and sister convinced Lady Huayang to grant him an audience. At the ensuing meeting, Lü Buwei pointedly reminded Lady Huayang that the current King of Qin was seventy years old and her husband the Crown Prince would ascend to the throne soon. When her husband became king, he would have to name an heir. That meant the status of the sonless Lady Huayang would deteriorate and her future well-being would be at risk. He then told her that Ying Yiren, one of her husband the Crown Prince's twenty sons who was stuck in the enemy state, thought about her every day and wished her peace and wellness. It would be his great honor and blessing to be her adopted son.

Most importantly, Ying Yiren's birth mother was of little importance and would not pose any threat to her, should she adopt him as a son. The adoption would make Ying Yiren "the eldest son of the main wife", and therefore the heir apparent to the Crown Prince. With her adopted son becoming the crown prince when the current Qin King died, and then the Qin King when her husband died, Lady Huayang's future would be secured. She would be destined to become the queen dowager.

This was an offer Lady Huayang could not refuse. So, with one masterstroke after another, Lü Buwei, despised by the ruling class and social elites, pulled off one of the most ingenuous and consequential deals in Chinese history. What made this possible was not just the practicalities of political math and the forces of supply and demand, but his strategic insight and understanding of human nature.

Ying Yiren might have been "the man who will be king", but he still had to stay in the enemy state as a hostage. One day, Ying Yiren went to Lü Buwei's home for a banquet. After a few drinks, the slightly intoxicated Ying Yiren was transfixed by the dancing performance of the merchant's concubine named Zhao Ji. Zhao Ji was said to be one of those women whom men could never forget once they had laid eyes on her. The suddenly emboldened Ying Yiren asked the host to let him have this woman. Lü Buwei was furious (some historians thought he was just putting on a show) but dutifully complied. Regardless of how sincere it was, Ying Yiren's request gave his host a blunt reminder of who the master was. As history would have it, Ying Yiren went on to have a child with Zhao Ji in the enemy state and the infant boy went on to become the First Emperor of China. Another historical account recorded that Zhao Ji had already been impregnated by Lü Buwei and hence the first Emperor was instead the merchant's child.[6]

In the meantime, the Qin state continued to clash on the battlefield with its main rival state (where Ying Yiren was residing) and scored one victory after another. The people in the enemy state wanted to kill Ying Yiren for revenge. The always resourceful Lü Buwei bribed the guards watching Ying Yiren and his young family, and the two men managed to escape back to Qin. Zhao Ji and her son, the future first Emperor of China, were left behind and had to hide from the furious citizens of the enemy state. Ying Yiren, like many successful men who came before and after him, felt no qualms about abandoning his family in pursuit of his political goals.

Upon his arrival at Qin, Ying Yiren strategically changed his name to Zichu (子楚) which literally meant he was a son of the Chu (楚) state from where Lady Huayang came. This was a clear demonstration of loyalty, as was his wearing of traditional clothing from Lady Huayang's homeland. Zhao Ji and her son, the future First Emperor of China, would have to spend a few more nerve-racking years in the enemy state before being escorted back to Qin.

The old king was soon to die and Ying Yiren's father, as crown prince, would become the new Qin King, who would also die a few months after ascending to the throne. Ying Yiren would assume the Qin throne. Keeping his promise, he made Lady Huayang the queen dowager. Nor did he forget his low-status biological mother, naming her the queen dowager as well. His household was now truly great, and he kept his end of the bargain by appointing Lü Bu Wei as the prime minister. Zhao Ji became the Qin Queen and her son with Ying Yiren became the crown prince.

---

[6]According to *The First Emperor's Biography* (秦始皇本纪) in Sima Qian's (司马迁) *Records of the Grand Historian* (史记), Qin Shihuang was conceived by Ying Yiren soon after he took Zhao Ji as concubine. However, in Lü Buwei's biography within the same book, Sima Qian wrote that Zhao Ji was already pregnant with Lü Buwei's child but the pregnancy was longer than usual and she later gave birth to Qin Shihuang. This was said to have been Lü Buwei's plan all along, to have his child become the Qin King and later to rule all of China. Since *Records of the Grand Historian* is the most prominent historical text for the ancient period and there are two versions of the story, one would have to wait till we open up Qin Shihuang's tomb and perform a DNA test to confirm his paternal identity.

THE MERCHANT'S FATE

Ying Yiren spent only three years on the throne before he died. His son Ying Zheng, later more popularly known as Qin Shihuang or the First Emperor of China, ascended to the throne as the King of Qin when he was only twelve. His mother Zhao Ji became queen dowager and Lü Buwei became the grand prime minister administering the state's affairs on behalf of the child emperor.

Lü Buwei at this point was at the highest point of his political career. To demonstrate his influence, he had over 3,000 scholars living as his guests in his mansion. They would co-author a book for their host titled *Master Lü's Spring and Autumn Annals* (吕氏春秋). A text on political philosophy, it proposes a softer version of Qin's iron-fisted, hard-nosed policies with elements borrowed from the laissez-faire tradition of the *Tao Te Ching* (道德经). Interestingly, early Han policymakers adopted certain ideas from *Master Lü's Spring and Autumn Annals* and one could not help but wonder if the Qin Dynasty, lasting only fifteen years, could have remained in power longer had it not controlled China with such a heavy hand. In any case, Lü Buwei was so proud of his book that he offered 1,000 pieces of gold for anyone who could find any flaw in the text or alter a word in it. Of course no one did. This illustrated not only his hubris but also his power. Who would dare to challenge a book written by the grand prime minister?

However, there was one major problem that Lü Buwei had to deal with. His old lover, the queen dowager Zhao Ji, was a widow in her thirties and the two rekindled their desires for each other. Normally, all men who lived in the palace, apart from the emperor and the young princes, had to be castrated. But as prime minister, Lü Buwei had the privilege of entering the palace without being scrutinized.

As Ying Zheng was getting older and was no longer a child, Lü Buwei was worried that the king would find out about his dangerous liaison with his mother. Lü Buwei, with usual moral and tactical dexterity, decided to seek outside help. This he found in a physically strong person[7] whose manhood, according to *Records of the Grand Historian*, was so well-endowed that it could spin wheels. Wheels in this case were the heavy structures for ancient Chinese carts. This account must have been particularly painful for the author of *Records of the Grand Historian* to write as he himself had been castrated by the emperor of his time for speaking up for a general who had defected to the northern nomads. The historian chose such a punishment over death as he had to complete his magnum

---

[7]The strong man was named Lao Ai (嫪毐) who became a guest at Lü Buwei's mansion after the prime minister knew about his endowment.

opus. In any case, the master manipulator Lü Buwei let the queen dowager Zhao Ji in on the strong man's sexual prowess, and she immediately found a place for him in her palace where she could have exclusive access to his "service".

For the strong man to enter the palace, he must at least be known to have become a eunuch. Lü Buwei staged a scene in which the strong man harassed a woman and the punishment for that crime was castration. A fake operation was then performed on him and he had to pluck out his beard to make himself look the part. He entered the queen dowager Zhao Ji's palace and very soon they had two children together. He was granted the rank of Marquis, a title which in Qin was reserved for people with military accomplishments.

The strong man, now the queen dowager Zhao Ji's lover and a Marquis, became increasingly ambitious. Trying to emulate Lü Buwei, he took in 1,000 guests at his mansion. Lü Buwei was known as the "lesser father" to Ying Zheng for all that he had accomplished for Ying Yiren. It was a title of honor indicating how important Lü Buwei was to the regime. Perhaps blinded by jealousy, the strong man gave himself the title "fake father" to the young king. There was nothing honorable about this title which implied a sexual relationship between him and the queen dowager Zhao Ji. The possibility that Ying Zheng, at the doorstep of adulthood, would find out about the affair grew with each passing day. The strong man decided to strike preemptively. In ancient times, an individual would be recognized as an adult when he turned twenty-two. As a rite of passage, he would attend a ceremony of putting his hair up to form a bun like a crown. As Ying Zheng's coming of age ceremony was scheduled to take place shortly outside the capital, the strong man plotted to stage a coup d'état during his absence.

However, the strong man was punching beyond his weight class in trying to take on Ying Zheng and found himself surrounded by the young king's army. The strong man's revolt was duly put down and he was executed by the method of "death by five horses" where the subject's head and limbs were tied to five horses and the beasts were made to run in each direction till the body was ripped into five pieces. The two children that the strong man had with the queen dowager, half-brothers of Ying Zheng, were put into a large bag and thrown to the ground repeatedly till they died. The queen dowager was put under house arrest and the young king made it clear that anyone who would speak up for her was to be executed. This, however, did not prevent twenty-seven officials from doing so and they were all killed. A twenty-eighth individual tempted fate and pleaded for the queen dowager. Unlike his unfortunate predecessors, however, this gentleman did not approach the situation from a moralistic viewpoint. Instead, he advised Ying

Zheng that if he were to unite the country, he had to stop alienating other vassal states and giving himself a bad name by treating his mother harshly. Ying Zheng was completely sold on the idea. After all, it was his lifelong ambition to give unity to the divided country. Not only did he free his mother from house arrest, he rewarded this empathetic adviser handsomely and with great honors.

Not long after the death of the strong man, Ying Zheng came to know that his lesser father Lü Buwei had been pulling the strings behind the whole affair all along. Without missing a beat, he stripped Lü Buwei of all his responsibilities and sent him back to his granted lands. Situated in the middle of China, the city was close to other vassal states whose ambassadors started visiting the former prime minister with offers for him to be their prime ministers. This got the attention of Ying Zheng, who banished Lü Buwei and his family to a more remote area, far away from all the other vassal states. Still worried, the young king decided to solve the problem once and for all by ordering Lü Buwei to commit suicide, thus fulfilling Lü Buwei's father's prophecy that putting a man to the throne would earn his son great fame and fortune but would also lead to his demise.

ANALYSIS

The success of Ying Yiren is best understood in the light of what Sun Tzu says on weaknesses and strengths in Chapter Six of *The Art of War* — "Water shapes its course according to the nature of the ground over which it flows; the soldier works out his victory in relation to the foe whom he is facing." This principle resonates with a parable told by Chuang Tzu (庄子), the Taoist philosopher, in which a butcher tells the king that the best chefs need to change their knives every year due to wear and tear while he has been using the same one for nineteen years. That is because he always takes the path of least resistance in accordance with the cow's anatomy.

By understanding the brilliance of Lü Buwei's proposal and flawless execution of strategy, Ying Yiren succeeded by taking the path of least resistance. Acting like water, he seized control of the Qin State almost effortlessly. In an attempt to do the same but with little success, Qin's rival states would have to exhaust their manpower and seek the advice of great thinkers. What Ying Yiren did, instead, was to make use of Lü Buwei's business acumen and the influence of the inner court to mobilize the entire Qin state to his advantage. Seen from this perspective, the Qin state was the cow, Ying Yiren the butcher, and the merchant his knife.

It is also worth noting that within the royal family in ancient China, weakness could be turned into strength. Ying Yiren's mother was a consort with no status. Had she been her husband's second most favorite consort, Lady Huayang would almost certainly have refused to take Ying Yiren as her adopted son. Once Lady Huayang had made up her mind, Ying Yiren proved himself to be her dutiful son by renaming himself as her state's child and wearing her native land's clothing. Between his biological and adoptive mothers, it was clear where Ying Yiren's loyalty resided. Adjusting the direction of one's sails in order to take advantage of the political winds had always been the key ingredient of success for the navigators of power games in Chinese history: Ying Yiren was a master navigator.

Turning to Lü Buwei, his brilliance was self-evident in his ability to pinpoint where there was most leverage in China's political environment at the time: the succession process to the throne of the Qin state, the most powerful regime then. His ability to persuade his counterparties was close to perfection and his execution flawless. However, his fate was predicted by his less accomplished but wiser father at the dawn of his political career. When one was involved in a game with the royal family, the stakes were beyond anything a merchant could have imagined. The accounting of imperial politics does not reward one with kindness, honors, and generosity based on how much he had achieved for the one in power.

Without Lü Buwei, Ying Zheng's father Ying Yiren would not have had a chance to be the king of Qin. In fact, without Lü Buwei, Ying Zheng's parents would not have even met. Maybe Lü Buwei was actually the father of Ying Zheng. However, that meant very little when it was time for the young king to decide Lü Buwei's fate. The former merchant was too powerful in the Qin state and his abilities were so great that if he were to work for any other regime, it would pose a great threat to Ying Zheng's own regime. The fact that he introduced the strong man to the queen dowager Zhao Ji, thus bringing much shame to the Qin royal household, did not help. The ruler, when deciding what to do with an official, rarely took into account what the individual had done for him. The only calculation for the one in power was whether that person was useful for his regime at the time and also the future.

An old Chinese adage summarizes it all,

"When the hares are hunted, you cook your hunting dog;
when all the birds are shot down, you store your bow."[8]

---

[8]The original saying in Chinese is as follows: 狡兔死, 走狗烹; 飞鸟尽、良弓藏。

Lü Buwei's purpose for the Qin state was complete and he was a greater liability and threat than an asset near the end of his life; hence Ying Zheng's rational decision to remove him from the mortal world. The birds and the rabbits are gone, there is no need for the tools to be kept around. Many generals and ministers would naively fall into the same trap as Lü Buwei in the millennia to come, hoping that their sacrifices for their rulers and regimes would earn them some mercy when crunch time came. No, rarely is such humanistic kindness shown in the entirety of Chinese imperial history.

CHAPTER 2

Fourth Prince Liu Heng

Lü Zhi

Liu Bang
(Founder of Han Dynasty)

Qi Ji

Bo Ji

Liu Ying
(Crown Prince/Emperor Of Han)

Liu Ruyi
(Third Prince)

LIU HENG
(Fourth Prince/
Emperor Of Han)

Chapter 2

Liu Heng: The Seasoned Card Player

Dynasty: Han (汉)

Period: circa 220 BC to 180 BC

Key Players:

Han Gaozu Liu Bang (汉高祖刘邦)**:** First Emperor of Han with the title Han Gaozu (汉高祖)

Lü Zhi (吕雉)**:** Liu Bang's wife, Empress, later Empress Dowager

Han Huidi Liuying (汉惠帝刘盈)**:** Son of Liu Bang and Lü Zhi, the Crown Prince, later Emperor of Han with the title Han Huidi (汉惠帝)

Qi Ji (戚姬)**:** Liu Bang's favorite Consort, mother of the third prince

Liu Ruyi (刘如意)**:** Son of Liu Bang and Qi Ji, the third prince

Bo Ji (薄姬)**:** Liu Bang's Consort, mother of the fourth prince

Han Wendi Liu Heng (汉文帝刘恒)**:** Son of Liu Bang and Bo Ji, the fourth prince, later Emperor with the title Han Wendi (汉文帝)

> *"In military combat, what is most difficult is turning the circuitous into the straight and adversity into advantage."*

> The Art of War, Chapter 7
> 《军争之难者，以迂为直，以患为利。》
> 孙子兵法第七章

HISTORICAL CONTEXT

The Qin Dynasty came to an abrupt end after fifteen years and China would be united again under the first emperor of the Han Dynasty, Liu Bang. Han turned out to be one of the longest-reigning dynasties in Chinese history whose nearly 400 years of rule ushered in the era of Imperial China.[1] How its founder and first emperor Liu Bang selected his heir would have far-reaching consequences for Chinese history.

LÜ ZHI — THE MAKING OF A MONSTER

Before he became a charismatic bandit leader, Liu Bang was a middle-aged man with little accomplishments and a strong appetite for alcohol. He was a small-time official in the local community, though his easy-going personality had won him many friends. He made the acquaintance of a rich gentleman who could do face reading. Convinced that Liu Bang would achieve great fame and fortune in the future, he insisted on marrying his oldest daughter Lü Zhi to the much older and socially inferior Liu Bang.[2] When the dutiful daughter set foot in Liu Bang's

---

[1] The Han Dynasty ruled China for about 400 years (202 BC–220 AD) with a brief interruption of the Xin Dynasty (新朝) (9–23 AD) in between. The First Han Dynasty (202 BC–9 AD) was known as the Western Han as the Capital was Chang'an (长安), modern day Xi'an (西安), while the Second Han Dynasty (23–220 AD) was known as the Eastern Han as its capital was in Luoyang (洛阳) which is located east of Xian.

[2] The gentleman's name was Lü Gong (吕公). He had come into conflict with a local despotic landlord and had to flee from his hometown. He had just arrived at Liu Bang's area, Pei (沛县) as he had an old friend that was an official there. To commemorate the arrival of an important person, the local official threw a banquet in his honor. The entry fee was 1,000 coins and Liu Bang, loving alcohol and lacking in shame, shouted that he was to pay 10,000 coins. The crowd was shocked, but no one really verified if Liu Bang had really paid the fee as the ticket check was run by his good friend Xiao He (萧何). Xiao He would proceed to be Liu Bang's main aide and first prime minister of the Han dynasty.

household, she was shocked to discover that her husband had been romantically involved with a widow and that the two had a son.[3]

Nevertheless, that did not stop Lü Zhi from performing her duties as Liu Bang's wife, which included working on the farm field to support the family. She even took care of Liu Bang's son and bore him a daughter and a son. On a prisoner escort mission, the accident-prone and absent-minded Liu Bang let half of the prisoners give him the slip. He then decided that he should throw himself into the spirit of things by letting the other half go. The prisoners, however, fell under his spell and became his followers. As negligence of duty by an official was a serious crime, Liu Bang had to flee and ended up becoming a bandit leader in the countryside.

From then on, Liu Bang and Lü Zhi would be separated for seven years. Left behind by her fugitive husband, Lü Zhi was thrown into prison for her husband's crimes. No written record was kept regarding her life behind bars, but we know that an upright prison guard would, out of righteous anger, severely punish his colleagues for torturing Lü Zhi.[4] Liu Bang joined the rebel force against the Qin regime which went from strength to strength, finally toppling the empire. His success was a thorn in the side of a formidable warrior who commanded the strongest military force against Qin at the time and named himself the "Overlord"[5] of all vassal regimes.

He was one of the three most important officials responsible for the establishment of the Han Dynasty (汉初三杰).

[3] Liu Bang had had an unofficial relationship with (maybe) a widow named Cao (曹) and they had a son between them, the future first prince Liu Fei (刘肥).

[4] The prison guard's name was Ren Ao (任敖). Due to the favor he did for Lü Zhi, Ren Ao would later become the vice prime minister of the Han regime; sometimes, though not often, standing up for justice pays.

[5] The Overlord's name was Xiang Yu (项羽). He was a young nobleman from the former vassal state Chu (楚) and he commanded the strongest military force against Qin at the time. Liu Bang, knowing that he was no match against Xiang Yu, voluntarily offered the Qin state, which he had captured, to him. Most of Xiang Yu's aides advised him to kill Liu Bang, but Xiang Yu was fearful of the reputational effects of murdering his erstwhile revolutionary comrade. By then, Xiang Yu was the most powerful military and political force in China and his vision was to have the country return to the pre-imperial order of a collection of vassal states. He named himself *Xichu Bawang* (西楚霸王 or the Overlord King of Western Chu) and granted lands to various lords, mostly descendants of former vassal state royalty, to create their own dominions. Liu Bang was given the remote land of Han (汉) in the southwest for fear of his ambition. Upon settling state matters, Xiang Yu returned to his hometown Peng (彭城) in the East of what is now Jiangsu province and built his capital which was only 200 miles (*Li*, 里) from Liu Bang's hometown, Pei (沛县).

Liu Bang, who harbored hopes of unifying China himself, rebelled against the Overlord and launched an attack on his capital. Despite its proximity to his hometown, he was more interested in looting the city than saving his family. When the Overlord counter-attacked, Liu Bang fled, leaving his wife and his father behind to become hostages. With the enemy army hot on his trail, Liu Bang tried to throw his children out of the wagon, all for the sake of "travelling light". If it had not been for his loyal driver, who pulled them back, the future first princess and Han emperor would almost certainly have perished. The Overlord, holding Liu Bang's father and Lü Zhi as hostages, negotiated on the battlefield with Liu Bang. He boiled water in a large pot and shouted to Liu Bang that if he did not surrender, he would cook his father and Lü Zhi alive. To which Liu Bang replied that since they had once called each other brothers, his father would also be the Overlord's father. If the Overlord decided to eat his own father, he should save a portion for him. The Overlord's ministers, alarmed and worried about the good name of their master, advised against killing the old man. In the end, the shamelessness of Liu Bang got the better of the Overlord's pride and self-respect.

LÜ ZHI'S EARLY ACTIONS AS EMPRESS

The Overlord eventually released the two hostages and Lü Zhi was able to reunite with Liu Bang. Having suffered so much for her husband, Lü Zhi was looking forward to a happy marriage. Reality would bitterly disappoint her. Liu Bang had been smitten by the love of his life, the young and beautiful Qi Ji. Not only was Qi Ji physically attractive, she was also an accomplished dancer. This complemented Liu Bang's musical talent — the Han Emperor was known to play instruments and sang songs that he composed himself on different occasions. They had a son named Ruyi, whose name meant "according to one's wish". In ancient China, the father's love for the son was usually a function of the love he had for his mother.

On the battlefield, the Overlord ultimately lost to Liu Bang who became the first emperor of the Han Dynasty. Despite his love for Qi Ji, Liu Bang made Lü Zhi the empress and their son Liu Ying the Crown Prince. How psychologically damaged and politically astute Lü Zhi emerged from her traumatic experience could be seen in the way she disposed of the two generals who had helped her husband unite the country. In the eyes of the empress, any potential threat challenging the absolute power of the emperor must be eliminated.

It has been said that there is a correlation between people's traumatic experiences and their subsequent cruelty as summarized in the phrase: hurt people hurt people. Lü Zhi's behavior after she became empress of the First Emperor of Han seems to lend validity to this postulation. One of the key figures who assisted Liu Bang in defeating Overlord was a great field marshal.[6] However, despite or perhaps because of his military laurels, the field marshal was perceived to be a threat by Liu Bang who put him under semi-house arrest in the capital. That was deemed too mild a measure for Lü Zhi, who joined hands with the prime minister to have the field marshal arrested with trumped-up charges. Then he was executed along with his "three tribes", meaning the extended families of his father, his mother and his wife. Ever the faithful wife mindful of her husband's good name, Lü Zhi made her move against the field marshal while Liu Bang was away from the capital in a battlefield putting down another revolt.

Another general[7] who helped Liu Bang defeat his nemesis, the Overlord, by attacking his army from behind was a guerrilla general. Regarded as another major threat by Liu Bang, the general was banished to a remote land. On his way to his land of exile, the general passed by the capital and made the fatal mistake of pleading with the Empress Lü Zhi for mercy. Not one to believe in leniency, Lü Zhi convinced Liu Bang that the general was still way too strong and influential to be kept alive. He was duly executed with his 3 tribes. The general's body was then made into a bolognese and distributed to the vassal state lords; most were generals who had assisted in Liu Bang's conquest of China. To prove their loyalty, the lords were required to finish eating the flesh under the surveillance of the emperor's messenger.

BO JI'S MISFORTUNE AND GOOD FORTUNE

Like other emperors in imperial China, Liu Bang, apart from Lü Zhi and Qi Ji, had many other women. One of them was Bo Ji, the descendant of the royal family of a vassal state. During the war of unification, Bo Ji was a consort in her own state which had pledged its loyalty to Liu Bang. Not long afterwards, Bo Ji's

---

[6] The field marshal was Han Xin (韩信). Of noble birth, he was responsible for most of the major campaigns that led to Liu Bang's establishment of the Han Dynasty. He was one of the three most important officials responsible for the establishment of the Han Dynasty (汉初三杰).

[7] The general's name was Peng Yue (彭越). He rose against Xiang Yu because he did not think he had received a fair share for his efforts in overthrowing the Qin Dynasty.

husband defected to the Overlord and Liu Bang sent his troops to punish the traitor. Bo Ji's home state soon fell and she was taken as hostage along with members of the royal family. Subsequently, she became a fabrics servant in Liu Bang's palace. One day, Liu Bang walked past the fabrics quarters and found Bo Ji to be quite attractive. However, there must have been a lot of distractions for the emperor did not send for her after this brief encounter. When he finally granted her the favor, it was not out of desire but an act of generosity.

As it happened, Bo Ji was a good friend of Liu Bang's two favorite consorts. After they had entered the palace, they made a pact that whoever was favored by the Emperor first would recommend the others to His Majesty. When the two consorts told Liu Bang about this, the Emperor summoned Bo Ji to his palace and the former fabrics lady told him about her dream in which a dragon sat on top of her stomach. Liu Bang then proceeded to make her dream come true.

Liu Bang would not see Bo Ji again, but that one time was enough for her to bear the Emperor a child, his fourth son named Liu Heng. As his mother Bo Ji had never meant anything to Liu Bang, Liu Heng was made the vassal king of a remote and poor land in the North.[8] Since Bo Ji had been practically ignored by Liu Bang, she was never perceived as a threat by Lü Zhi, who allowed her to go to the vassal kingdom to unite with her son Liu Heng.

TWO MOTHERS' FIGHT FOR THEIR SONS' STATUS TO BE HEIR

While busy helping her husband to consolidate his power, Lü Zhi also had to work to protect her own position and strengthen her son Liu Ying's status. At the same time, the emperor's favorite concubine Qi Ji, leveraging Liu Bang's love for her, schemed to make her son the third prince Liu Ruyi replace the incumbent crown prince. Liu Bang called a meeting with the top officials[9] to discuss the issue and they argued there were strong reasons to why the heir to the throne was often referred to as the "foundation of the regime". To change the crown prince was to shake the empire to its foundations. Lü Zhi was listening in the back and as soon as the officials came out of the meeting, she got down on one knee and thanked them for speaking up for her son.

---

[8] Dai (代) was a remote and poor land in modern day northern Shanxi (山西) close to Inner Mongolia (内蒙古)

[9] Present was one of the earliest followers of Liu Bang named Zhou Chang (周昌). He had a serious case of stuttering but nonetheless spoke out against Liu Bang's intention to change the crown prince.

The embattled Lü Zhi then turned to one of Liu Bang's key strategic advisors[10] for help. He told her that there were four old reputable gentlemen who had been living in the mountains and had refused Liu Bang's invitation to join the government. If Lü Zhi was able to convince them to show support to Liu Ying, the crown prince's status would be guaranteed. The four old gentlemen were reluctant at first but eventually they were won over by the persistence and persuasiveness of Lü Zhi. They also understood the importance of securing the foundation of the empire. As a show of support to the Crown Prince, they travelled all the way to the palace and walked behind the crown prince Liu Ying as they entered. That was enough for the Emperor to change his mind about naming a new crown prince. Instead, he made Qi Ji's son, the third prince Liu Ruyi, a vassal king of a prosperous region.[11]

THE FATE OF QI JI AND LIU RUYI

After Liu Bang's death, Liu Ying assumed the throne and Lü Zhi became the empress dowager. As Liu Ying was still a teenager, de facto power rested with his mother Lü Zhi. True to form, she quickly moved to torture her nemesis Qi Ji. She ordered for Qi Ji's head to be shaved and had her neck locked with a heavy wooden block. Though her son the third prince was a vassal king, Qi Ji was not excluded from forced labor and had to plant crops all day.

The musically talented Qi Ji expressed her grievances in a song that went:

"The son is a king; the mother is a slave!

Spending her days planting crops, death is always near her!

Mother and Son are so far apart! Who is there to tell him of my situation?"[12]

When Lü Zhi found out about the song, she was furious and summoned the third prince to the capital. Against the advice of his prime minister[13] and his own

---

[10]The key advisor was Zhang Liang (张良), who was responsible for mapping out the key strategic maneuvers for Liu Bang in the process of unifying China. He was one of the three most important officials responsible for the establishment of the Han Dynasty (汉初三杰)

[11]The vassal kingdom was named Zhao (赵) in what is modern day Hebei (河北) and Shanxi (山西). It was a relatively fertile land back in the early Han period.

[12]The song in its original Chinese is as follows: 子為王，母為虜！終日舂薄暮，常與死相伍！相離三千里！誰當使告汝！

[13]Being a shrewd and experienced politician, Liu Bang made Zhou Chang, the person who spoke out in support of Liu Ying, the prime minister of Zhao. In Liu Bang's calculations,

better judgment, the third prince complied, and his life was temporarily spared only by the intervention of his older brother Liu Ying, now the emperor. The Emperor tried to keep the third prince in sight at all times, knowing that his brother would very likely be murdered in his absence. One morning, he went out hunting and left his younger brother who was too lazy to get up in bed. When he came back, his brother had already died of poisoning.

After disposing of the son, Lü Zhi proceeded to make her move against his mother Qi Ji. She had her rival's limbs removed, took out her eyes, poked through her ear drums, cut off her tongue and threw her into the toilet. Then she asked her son the emperor Liu Ying to come over and check out "the creature" whom she gleefully referred to as a human pig. The Emperor was devastated and wondered how he could possibly be the ruler of all the people under heaven with a mother who was so brutal. From then on, he went into a downward spiral of self-destruction, indulged in alcoholism, and withdrew from state affairs.

LÜ ZHI'S TREATMENT OF LIU BANG'S OTHER SONS

With Liu Ying's rapid decline, Lü Zhi tightened her grip on the Han regime. Her husband Liu Bang, while in power, managed to get rid of all the vassal kings who had assisted him in the founding of the empire, and replaced them with his own sons. By doing so, he tried to learn from the mistakes made by his predecessors. It was widely believed that the Qin dynasty had fallen so quickly because none of its regional officials came from the royal household and therefore they had little incentive to defend the empire against revolts. Liu Bang also had his top officials make a pact with him — no one whose last name was not Liu would ever be given the title of vassal king again. He commemorated the event by killing a white horse and hence the pact was known as "The Covenant of the White Horse".

Many of Liu Bang's sons perished under Lü Zhi.[14] The one who survived was the self-effacing fourth prince Liu Heng. After the murder of the third prince, his

---

Zhou Chang earned a huge favor from Lü Zhi and Liu Ying and would be able to protect Liu Ruyi in his position as the vassal king of Zhao. Liu Bang would be wrong and Zhou Chang would later die out of anger and sorrow as he thought he had let Liu Bang and third prince Liu Ruyi down.

[14] One fortunate exception was Liu Bang's eldest son Liu Fei, whom the Emperor had before Lü Zhi was married to him. Liu Bang conferred to his eldest son the title of the king of Qi (齐), which was a fertile piece of land situated in modern day Shandong (山东). Vassal kings had the duty of visiting the capital on a regular basis and Liu Fei was no exception. Once, when Liu Fei visited the capital, the emperor Liu Ying threw a banquet

vassal state was given to two other sons of Liu Bang successively. Neither of them, however, got along with their wives, who were both nieces of Lü Zhi. The Empress Dowager, always one to take things personally, had the two men killed.[15] With the throne of the vassal state empty again, Lü Zhi named the fourth prince its new lord. The fourth prince was then the king of a much more remote and poorer vassal state, indicative of the lack of affection his father Liu Bang had for his mother Bo Ji. Having observed the downfall of his many brothers, especially his third brother Liu Ruyi, the fourth prince shrewdly told Lü Zhi that he would rather be the defender of the northern border than live a life of luxury in a more prosperous vassal state. Pleased with his answer, Lü Zhi decided to leave the fourth prince alone and he would go on to survive this era of political turmoil.

THE OUTER RELATIVES BECAME THE INNER CIRCLE

Suffering from depression and alcoholism, Lü Zhi's son Liu Ying died at the age of twenty-four, seven years after assuming the throne. Lü Zhi retained her control by making one of Liu Ying's young sons the child emperor. As expected, she then

---

in honor of his older brother. The brothers had a good relationship and became a little too casual with each other. During the banquet, Liu Ying allowed his older brother to take his seat, the equivalent of treason under traditional Confucian court rules. Lü Zhi, unhappy about this and also feeling the threat of Liu Fei, demanded Liu Fei to toast to her. She ordered the wine to be poisoned and when Liu Fei took a cup to toast Lü Zhi, the emperor Liu Ying, out of joy, took a cup to toast as well. Unsure which cup was poisoned, Lü Zhi snapped Liu Ying's cup out of his hand. Liu Fei knew that Lü Zhi had tried to poison him and so he remained humble until he could leave for his vassal state Qi. Upon his return, Liu Fei allocated ten out of a total of seventy cities of Qi for Lü Zhi's daughter. Out of submission to Lü Zhi, he named Lü Zhi's daughter the empress dowager of the state of Qi. Liu Fei was in actuality calling his own half younger sister (Lü Zhi's daughter) his own mother (empress dowager of his own state). These gestures of total capitulation on the part of Liu Fei to Lü Zhi would allow him to live the rest of life in relative peace.

[15] Liu Bang's other son Liu You (刘友) was named the king of Zhao after the death of Liu Ruyi. Lü Zhi ordered him to marry a niece of hers from the Lü clan. The pair did not get along and Liu You's wife reported to Lü Zhi that her husband was plotting to rebel against the central government. Liu You was brought to the capital Chang'an and was starved to death while in custody. Another of Liu Bang's sons Liu Hui (刘恢) took up the role of the king of Zhao after his brother's death. He also married a niece of Lü Zhi from the Lü clan. Like his brother before him, he did not get along with his wife and instead was deeply in love with his favorite concubine. His wife would have none of that and ordered for the murder of the concubine. Sad beyond words, Liu Hui committed suicide.

killed the mother of the child emperor for fear of her having any influence on him. When the emperor grew up and learned of his mother's fate, he vowed to take revenge. This left Lü Zhi with little choice. She put her own grandson the emperor in confinement and installed another of Liu Ying's sons as the new child emperor.

Now at the peak of her power, Lü Zhi was still haunted by a deep sense of insecurity and was dismayed by the fact that the garrison stationed in the capital was not under her control. This was no trivial issue, for history had proved time and again that whoever controlled the army of the capital held the key to success in court struggles. With the support of the senior officials, she made her nephew the grand general and appointed another nephew as a key minister. They were then put in charge of the capital's army.[16] Lü Zhi also made them kings of vassal states, in direct violation of Liu Bang's policy that only descendants of the Liu clan would be given the title of vassal kings.

THE FALL OF THE LÜ CLAN AND THE RESTORATION OF EQUILIBRIUM

Due to incompetence and a lack of legitimacy, the Lü clan commanded little respect from members of the Liu royal family[17] and senior officials. Lü Zhi died under strange circumstances fifteen years after the death of her husband. One day while walking in the countryside, she was attacked by a black dog which might have given her rabies. She started to exhibit symptoms of the disease such as confusion, seizures, and hallucinations. Legend has it that the dog was the

---

[16] Lü Zhi made her nephew Lü Lu (吕禄) the grand general and appointed her other nephew Lü Chan (吕产) as a key minister. They were put in charge of the capital's army.

[17] One case illustrated the sentiment. Liu Zhang (刘章), the second son of Liu Fei, the King of Qi, was only twenty at the time when Lü Zhi made him the administrator of a royal banquet. Liu Zhang was talented as well as aggressive and Lü Zhi was quite fond of him. He said that he would administer the banquet with military level discipline, to which Lü Zhi agreed. When one member of the Lü clan complained that he was drunk and was leaving the banquet; Liu Zhang, stating that the Lü gentleman had left his military post, went ahead and killed him. Even though a member of the Lü family was murdered, it was Lü Zhi who agreed with the military administration of the banquet and as such, she could not reprimand Liu Zhang. As if the banquet was not eventful enough, Liu Zhang spiced things up by singing a song that went, "When one is planting crops, he must plant them deep and also leave enough space between them. One must pluck away the unwanted weeds." (深耕 穊种, 立苗欲疏, 非其种者, 锄而去之。) This was a direct verbal attack against Lü Zhi's raising of the Lü clan to high office.

reincarnation of the third prince coming back to avenge his mother and himself. In any case, Lü Zhi, even on her deathbed, moved to consolidate the power of her clan.

She put her nephews in charge of the capital's imperial army. The last order she gave was to stay put in their military posts. Under no circumstances should they leave, not even to attend her funeral. Lü Zhi died shortly afterwards and the demise of her maiden family happened as swiftly as the fall of domino cards. One month after Lü Zhi's death, members of the Liu royal family launched an attack on the capital.[18] Meanwhile, the top officials in the capital plotted to seize power from the widely despised Lü clan. They succeeded when the top general of the empire got hold of the military stamp from the young emperor and took over the command of the imperial army. Those who remained loyal to the Lü clan were either killed or arrested subsequently.[19]

---

[18] One month after Lü Zhi's death, the formidable Liu Zhang wrote to his older brother, Liu Xiang (刘襄), the king of Qi to rebel and attack the capital Chang'an. The two nephews of Lü Zhi commissioned the old general Guan Ying (灌婴) to put down the revolt. Guan Ying was one of Liu Bang's key generals who was ultimately loyal to the Liu family rather than to the nephews of Lü Zhi. With Lü Zhi gone, he had no real incentive to carry out the Lü clan's orders. He and his army stalled in modern day Henan (河南) which was halfway between the capital Chang'an in the west and Qi in the east. He was to wait for his long-term colleagues to execute their plan back in the capital city.

[19] Most of the top officials in Chang'an, led by the key ministers Chen Ping (陈平) and Zhou Bo (周勃) who had assisted Liu Bang in establishing the Han Dynasty, were uncompromising to the Lü clan's leadership and were plotting to eliminate them. However, the key military forces were officially in the hands of the Lü leaders. Chen Ping and Zhou Bo found a way to access the army by having Lü Lu's best friend Li Ji (郦寄) convince Lü Lu to give up his status of mastery over the capital's army for a peaceful return to his vassal state of Zhao to be king there. Lü Lu, unambitious and naïve, agreed to such a proposal. Zhou Bo, the Han regime's official top national military official, managed to get a hold of the military stamp from the young Emperor. He proceeded to enter into the northern army camp and asked the soldiers to show their left shoulder from their clothing if they were still loyal to Han's royal family of Liu or show their right shoulder instead if they would continue to follow the Lü Clan. Everyone in the camp showed their left shoulder and Zhao Bo took over the northern army accordingly. Not knowing that the northern army was already controlled by the high officials, Lü Chan brought a small number of soldiers from his southern army to the palace in the attempt to take control of the young emperor. The courageous Liu Zhang brought 1,000 soldiers from the northern army and won the fight against Lü Chan and his followers. He chased Lü Chan into the bathroom and had him killed there.

CHOOSING THE NEW EMPEROR

With the Lü clan out of the picture, a new power equilibrium would have to be established. The incumbent young emperor was chosen by Lü Zhi and therefore had to be replaced. At that time, the capital was controlled by the top officials who now played the role of kingmakers. They decided to pass over the sons of Liu Ying who were too young and had been too accommodating to Lü Zhi's wishes. The grandsons of Liu Bang deserved credit for overthrowing the Lü clan.[20] However, they were too formidable for the high officials' taste: the ministers wished to have someone they could control more easily and since the royal family was in shambles after the deeds of Lü Zhi, it was their chance to find an emperor who could safeguard their collective interest.

If the grandsons of Liu Bang were not to be chosen, what about his remaining sons, the fourth prince Liu Heng and the other prince raised by Lü Zhi?[21] Clearly the other prince was out of the running as his closeness to Lü Zhi aroused fear from the high officials who had removed the Lü clan from power. That left the fourth prince as the only possible choice. He was the vassal king of a faraway land with little influence in either the prosperous parts of the empire or the capital. Moreover, his mother Bo Ji, who would automatically become the empress dowager if her son was to assume the throne, had very humble beginnings. Her family, the Bo clan, was known to be uninterested in wealth and power. Therefore, the chances of developing a dominant outer relative faction like the Lü clan were slim. As a result, the fourth prince was named the emperor and invited to go to the capital to assume the throne.

Among his ministers and key advisers, opinions were divided over whether it was the throne or a trap waiting for the emperor in the capital. The fourth prince resorted to a mode of decision-making frequently used in ancient China in face of uncertainty and especially when the stakes were high: fortune telling. The results turned out to be overwhelmingly positive,[22] indicating that the person

---

[20] Liu Xiang, the powerful king of Qi who staged the uprising, could be a natural choice. He was the eldest son of the eldest son. Absent of choosing from Lü Zhi's main line of descent, this would make the most sense. Otherwise, Liu Xiang's young brother Liu Zhang, who was most responsible for eliminating the Lü clan, ought to be a powerful contender as well.

[21] This son of Liu Bang was Liu Chang (刘长) and had the misfortune of his mother dying early. He was lucky enough to be adopted by Lü Zhi herself which meant that he lived in peace during the period of her rule.

[22] The results turned out to be "The Great Horizontal" (大横) which was overwhelmingly positive and meant that the person asking was about to assume greatness.

asking for advice was about to assume greatness. It would be impossible to tell if this was in fact a divine message, though throughout history both in China and the West, omens were often fabricated by the ones in power to bestow legitimacy upon their actions or decisions. In ancient Rome, for example, Caesar would release doves to boost the confidence of his soldiers. Fabricated or not, the results of fortune telling definitely worked in the fourth prince's favor.

The fourth prince Liu Heng remained on high alert as he traveled towards the capital and would stall repeatedly and dispatched his trusted men to gather further intelligence.[23] He was finally received by the high officials in the outskirts of the capital and they bowed to their new emperor. Liu Heng reciprocated by paying them the same respects. The top general[24] wanted to meet with his new master in private but was told that where official matters were concerned, he should state his case in public. If the matter that he wished to discuss was personal, he was reminded that the emperor would not discuss personal matters for he was selfless. Having been put in his place, the powerful general gave the emperor's stamp, which represented imperial power, to its rightful owner Liu Heng.

Upon arriving at the capital, Liu Heng lost no time in fostering loyalty and building his power base. First, he sent two of his two confidants to take over the command of the army in the capital and its imperial guards. Then he ordered the execution of the young emperors and their brothers who had been granted titles by Lü Zhi. Giving them their dues, he appointed the key top officials as the right and left prime ministers respectively. Members of the royal family were rewarded with the titles of vassal kings. To put the succession system back on track, he named the eldest son of his empress as the Crown Prince, as appropriate under the traditional Chinese hereditary system.

The fourth prince Liu Heng, who had always kept his head low and flew under the radar of his enemies when out of power, applied the same humility and pragmatism to governing the country. Under his policy, which may be called positive non-intervention today, China's economy took off. Along with his son, he put China on a road towards its first golden age in the imperial era.

---

[23] Liu Heng sent his uncle Bo Zhao (薄昭) to the capital first to further understand the situation. When he was only fifty miles away from the capital Chang'an, he dispatched his main confidant Song Chang (宋昌) to arrive before him.

[24] The top general was Zhou Bo (周勃) who was the highest commander of the armed forces of the empire.

ANALYSIS

"In military combat what is most difficult is turning the circuitous into the straight, and adversity into advantage." This verse from chapter seven of *The Art of War* best describes how the fourth prince Liu Heng and his mother emerged as the ultimate winners from the royal family turmoil of this period.

Bo Ji, the fabrics lady, had neither beauty nor talent to win herself a place in the heart of her husband. In fact, she was so inconspicuous that she did not even appear on the radar of the eternally jealous Lü Zhi. As the great philosophical classic *Tao Te Ching* (道德经) reminds us, "Good fortune follows disaster; disaster lurks within good fortune". The emperor's indifference was a blessing in disguise for Bo Ji.

Her son's talent for turning adversity into advantage was even more pronounced. By refusing to be the king of a prosperous area, a title which had already cost the lives of a few princes, the fourth prince put himself out of harm's way. In doing so, he also announced to the world that he knew his place and would always act accordingly. Such was the reason why he was preferred to the ambitious, powerful Liu princes by the kingmakers. That his mother came from a humble background was also reassuring to the royal family and senior ministers. They did not have to worry about the outer relatives having too much power once the fourth prince ascended to the throne.

The new Emperor, however, was anything but a pushover. When the moment to take action came, he never failed to be decisive, even ruthless. Resorting to fortune-telling was not superstitious, but a shrewd political move that provided his ascendance to the throne with divine legitimacy. When he arrived at the capital, he acted so swiftly that it reminds one of how a leopard would behave for its kill. First, he had the many young emperors whose titles had been granted by Lü Zhi executed, thus eliminating any potential competition for the throne. Then he swiftly took over the control of the military force in the capital. In restoring the power equilibrium in court, he used carrots as effectively as he used sticks. High officials were granted titles while members of the royal family were rewarded with additional vassals and lands.

According to the great political philosopher in the late Warring States Period Han Feizi (韩非子), the ruler must not demonstrate his desires, lest it become leverage for his subjects. The ruler's thoughts and motives must remain unknown to the people around him. Those who worked for him, on the contrary, must be made to speak their minds and act accordingly. In other words, if imperial rule was a card game, the emperor should insist on seeing the cards of his ministers at all times while holding his own as close to his chest as possible.

That was exactly how Liu Heng had played his hand right from the start. He never appeared too eager for the job offered to him by the senior ministers in the capital. He knew in a power relationship, the one who had more to gain is also the one who had more to lose, and the one who wanted it less will be the one in control. Since the powers-that-be in the capital had concluded that his enthronement would serve their best interests, showing elusiveness and strategic ambiguity as to his true intentions would strengthen his bargaining position and tilt the power dynamics in his favor. That was why he was in no hurry to get to the capital to assume the throne and refused to talk to the top general in private.

His father Liu Bang, in contrast, was a much less accomplished card player in this context. He did the right thing when he followed tradition and named Liu Ying, his eldest son from his empress Lü Zhi, the crown prince. However, his indiscretion would cost him and his loved ones dearly when he failed to conceal his preference for his favorite concubine and their son. Due to the essential role high officials had played in its founding, the early Han Dynasty developed a system that required the emperor to share power with his ministers. By taking the side of Qi Ji and the third prince Liu Ruyi so obviously, Liu Bang unwittingly turned the mother and son into Lü Zhi's mortal enemies. This would seal their fate. Court politics did not take prisoners. You had to pay for your ambition and failure with your life.

As for the others in the story, both Qi Ji and Lü Zhi committed the fatal mistake of biting off more than they could chew. Naming the crown prince was the ultimate political act and power play, and a decision not even the emperor could make alone. Qi Ji's failure to understand this made it inevitable that she and her son would come to a bad end. Lü Zhi, though much more politically astute, fell into the same trap. Not satisfied with the power she had accumulated after Liu Bang's death, she strengthened her control of the regime by filling the various posts of the government with her relatives, while having little idea of how this would affect the vested interests in court and power equilibrium. The demise of the Lü's clan was almost guaranteed after her death. Despite everything Lü had done, the Han regime was still very much dominated by the senior officials whose influence was equally strong in the administrative and military spheres.

In Chapter Four of *The Art of War*, Sun Tzu says, "The winning general puts himself in a winning position first and then seeks battle." Qi Ji and Lü Zhi had done the exact opposite. That made them the losing players of the story.

First Prince Cao Pi

Cao Cao
(Founder of Wei Dynasty)

CAO PI
(First Prince/
Emperor Of Wei)

Cao Zhi
(Third Prince)

Chapter 3

Cao Pi & The Triumph
of the Good Son

Dynasty: 3 Kingdoms (三国) **/ Wei** (魏)

Period: circa 190 AD to 220 AD

Key Players:

Wei Wudi Cao Cao (魏武帝曹操): Effective founder of the Wei Dynasty with the title of Wei Wudi (魏武帝)

Wei Wendi Cao Pi (魏文帝曹丕): Eldest surviving son of Cao Cao, later Emperor of Wei with the title Wei Wendi (魏文帝)

Cao Zhi (曹植): Third eldest surviving son of Cao Cao, a towering figure in Chinese literature

"Attaining one hundred victories in one hundred battles is not the pinnacle of excellence. Subjugating the enemy's army without fighting is."

The Art of War, Chapter 3

《是故百战百胜，非善之善者也；不战而屈人之兵，善之善者也。》

孙子兵法第三章

HISTORICAL CONTEXT

The Han Dynasty (202 BC–220 AD) coincided with the golden days of the Roman Empire and, like its Western counterpart, fell into turmoil around the end of the second century. A long period of peace led to overpopulation and an increasing concentration of land ownership in the hands of a few. Moreover, the emperors of the Eastern Han Dynasty (23–220 AD) mostly died early.[1] Their successors were often so young that de facto power would be transferred to their mothers, the empress dowagers who themselves were often in their twenties, and their clans of outer relatives. Their unchecked influence would ultimately pose a serious threat to imperial power. As the empire fell into decline and the lives of the common people became increasingly difficult, its legitimacy was called into question. Outbreaks of violence against the government emerged all over the country.

At that time, the government bureaucracy was dominated by the gentry or literati. The gentry system through which scholars gained access to high government offices in the Han Dynasty was known as "Nominating the filially pious and uncorrupted" (举孝廉, or *ju xiao lian*). Each region of the empire would have esteemed gentlemen nominate young men who exhibited these traits to join the government. The system, almost by design, led to the emergence of the self-perpetuating gentry class whose members looked after the interests of one another. It would also decay into form without substance. A young man, for example, was nominated for government office because he showed filial piety by remaining celibate and staying in his father's tomb during the mourning period. However, it was soon exposed that he had fathered children during that time. In another case, an older brother was nominated because he demonstrated his magnanimous nature by giving a portion of his inheritance to his younger brother. When his younger brother returned the inheritance, it was his turn to get nominated.

---

[1] The average life expectancy of Eastern Han emperors was thirty compared to Western Han's mean of thirty-seven. Some historians speculate that measles was transmitted into northern China from a war captive from modern day Guangdong.

With a tumultuous court situation, a continued fall in the quality of governance, and over-population, the empire went into decline. To aggravate matters, government offices were sometimes sold to the highest bidder to help the cash-strapped regime. An opportunist[2] convinced the peasants that their hardships had their roots in the illegitimacy of rule by the Han court. The only way out was to believe in his religion "The Way of the Great Peace" (太平道) and overthrow the government. When harmony was restored, they would not be in hunger again. With the uprisers distinguishing themselves with yellow head wear, this revolution was known as the "Yellow Turban Rebellion." (黄巾之乱).

Due to the scale of the revolt, the central government had no choice but to allow regional governments to raise their own armies to put down the revolt. The uprisers were soon effectively eliminated but the regional governments, now with their own armies, began to act in defiance of the central authority and became warlords in their local areas. The fiercest of these generals was one from northwestern China. Five years after the start of the "Yellow Turban Rebellion", in the name of putting down unrest in the capital, he led troops into the city and kidnapped the young Emperor.[3]

Thus, this marked the effective end of the Han central government. The regional warlords formed an alliance against the northwestern warlord and China entered into the phase popularly known as the "The Three Kingdoms Period". This is one of the best-known history periods popularized by the historical novel *Romance of the Three Kingdoms* and numerous computer games in modern times.

THE RISE OF CAO CAO

Ushering the country into the Three Kingdoms Period by conquering northern China was the founder of the Wei dynasty Cao Cao. Cao Cao's father was the adopted son of one of the most powerful Eastern Han eunuchs. Through the court's purchasing program of government offices, Cao Cao's father became

---

[2]The opportunist was Zhang Jiao (张角). He gathered his influence by creating a Taoist religion for the poor and needy. Zhang Jiao would perform healing acts and his followers had to kneel and confess their sins before they were treated.

[3]The general's name was Dong Zhuo (董卓). Coming from the northwestern part of China, his forces included the militarily formidable Qiang people (羌人) who had threatened the Eastern Han Dynasty throughout its existence. He marched in and sacked the capital Luoyang (洛阳), deposed the then emperor, raised another young prince to the throne (later known as Han Xiandi (汉献帝)) and returned to his area of influence in Chang'an.

the top official in the military. This demonstrated the wealth of the Cao family as well as the extent of corruption in the late Han period. Money, however, might buy the Cao family's political power but not genuine respect. The Confucius scholars and gentry class who represented the highest echelon of society would always remember Cao Cao's grandfather as a eunuch and held Cao Cao in contempt. This would prove to be a thorn in the flesh for Cao Cao, even after he became the founder of the Wei regime.

Regardless of how the Cao family was viewed, its wealth and position in court allowed Cao Cao to be nominated as "filially pious and uncorrupted" and gained him access to the civil service. He went on to lead one of the military forces responsible for putting down the "Yellow Turban Rebellion" and joined the alliance to fight the northwestern warlord who would eventually be murdered by his adopted son. With the threat from the northwest gone, the country was up for grabs again. Always the opportunist, Cao Cao took the Han Emperor under his wing. Brushing aside charges that he was holding the emperor hostage, Cao Cao named himself the prime minister and took effective control of the Han court.

Cao Cao then achieved a string of military victories in the most prosperous areas in China at the time along the Yellow River. The apex of his career was when he won the battle against a powerful warlord and former friend[4] who controlled the most strategic lands in northern China. Cao Cao then made a bold attempt to unify the country by invading the lands in the south. He was met with fierce resistance in the southeastern area where a lot of the gentry fled to from the north. The local warlord who subsequently created one of the three kingdoms, sent his most trusted general to fight against Cao Cao's forces from the north. Cao Cao's army was defeated in the battle when the southeastern army took advantage of the direction of the wind to cause a major fire in Cao Cao's fleet.[5] Subsequently, Cao Cao retreated back to the central part of China. Another warlord then took advantage of Cao Cao's defeat and occupied the southwestern part of China.[6]

---

[4]Cao Cao won the Battle of Guandu (官渡之战) (200 AD) against Yuan Shao (袁绍), a leader who possessed a lineage which would put him at the apex of the gentry.

[5]The local warlord was Sun Quan (孙权), who subsequently created one of the three kingdoms of Wu (吴). His army was led by the great general Zhou Yu (周瑜) and defeated Cao Cao's fleet at the Battle of Chibi (赤壁之战) (208 AD).

[6]Liu Bei (刘备), a self-proclaimed descendant from the royal Liu household of the Han Dynasty, utilized the power vacuum and took over the southwestern area named Shu (蜀), which is modern day Sichuan.

The country was thus divided into three separate centers of powers and the period was hence dubbed the "Three Kingdoms Period". Despite his fleet being burnt, Cao Cao remained the predominant force; controlling the most prosperous area of northern China. In a census done during the Three Kingdoms Period, for example, the Wei regime founded by Cao Cao had a population of 4.45 million, while the other two regimes had populations of 2.1 million and 0.94 million respectively. In other words, Cao Cao controlled around 60% of China's population and was therefore the dominant regime in China at the time.

Cao Cao saw improving the country's infrastructure as a means to increase its agricultural productivity. He refrained from waging further wars against his rivals and instead focused on irrigation building. There was a delicious irony to savor here. Cao Cao would persist in his efforts to build the agricultural infra-structure in the homeland of the general who burnt his fleet, which had fallen under Cao Cao's jurisdiction. Meanwhile, the southeastern warlord, the man for whom the general had given his life, would keep sending forces to attack the area. In his twilight years when he became convinced that the south would not be a part of the Wei's empire during his lifetime, Cao Cao, as the King of Wei and in control of the Han court with his daughter as the Empress, had to decide how his regime would survive beyond him.

The success of Cao Cao can be attributed to his ability to recognize and uti-lize talent. In the beginning of his tenure as a warlord, he issued an edict and declared that he would retain anyone based "purely on talent" (唯才是用, or *wei cai shi yong*). This stood in stark contrast to the Han way of "nominating the filially pious and uncorrupted". Ever the practical man, Cao Cao knew that, in the many wars that he would have to fight against other warlords, it was solid skills and not moral virtues that would help him win. This had important political impli-cations as the Eastern Han nomination system was designed to protect the trans-generational interests of the gentry families. By shifting the emphasis to practical skills, Cao Cao tried to puncture a hole in the monopoly on power by the scholarly aristocracy.

This proved to be a mission impossible even for Cao Cao, whose vision, resourcefulness, and force of personality made him a towering figure in Chinese history. The grip of the gentry on the Eastern Han court and politics was so tight that not even the chaos of a war-ravaged country could loosen it. It was no acci-dent that Cao Cao's main rivals in the south were members of the gentry class. Many of the generals and strategists of Cao Cao's rival regimes were noblemen who fled from the north during the "Yellow Turban Rebellion" and settled in the relatively peaceful Southern regions. Most of them were unwilling to be part of the empire built by an individual with a shameful family origin who ostensibly was holding the Emperor hostage.[7]

The challenge to Cao Cao's Wei regime did not only come from the south; but also from within his own camp. Due to his background of being from a eunuch family, Cao Cao was looked down upon by the gentry in his own jurisdiction. Having the emperor by his side should have given his regime the legitimacy and moral authority of the central government. However, it also meant that he could never be sure if his subjects were loyal to him or to the emperor and the Han regime. That was probably why he was reluctant to dethrone the emperor and take the reins himself. Instead, he settled for the title of King of Wei.

Cao Cao, though powerful, had many detractors. For example, a gentleman who was from a highly esteemed aristocratic family,[8] was one of Cao Cao's most trusted advisors. But he earned Cao Cao's ill will by fiercely resisting his rise within the Han court. The gentleman would eventually take his own life when Cao Cao was supposed to give him a set of expensive presents but gave him an empty box in lieu, implying that he was useless to Cao Cao. The aristocratic gentleman took the hint and duly committed suicide.

Another example was a famous scholar and the descendent of Confucius.[9] Uncomfortable with how Cao Cao was threatening the authority of the Han

---

[7] Cao Cao's main rivals in the south, Liu Bei and Sun Quan, were members of the Han royal family and the gentry class respectively who came from the north. Moreover, the main aides who supported their regimes were also from the same echelon of society. Zhuge Liang (诸葛亮), the famous prime minister under Liu Bei who was semi-deified by *Romance of The Three Kingdoms*, was from a prominent family in Shandong. Zhou Yu and Lu Su (鲁肃), the military men supporting Sun Quan were members of the gentry class as well. All of these gentlemen fled from the north to the south when central China fell into turmoil.

[8] The gentleman was Xun Yu (荀彧), who was one of the earliest followers of Cao Cao before he became a major warlord. Coming from an aristocratic family, Xun Yu's uncle was of the prime ministerial rank. Xun Yu was ultimately loyal to the Han Dynasty rather than Cao Cao's Wei Dynasty.

[9] The man was called Kong Rong (孔融), who rose to fame when he was only four years old. A direct descendant of Confucius, Kong Rong was so compliant with the Confucian ideals of familial piety at such a young age that when given a choice of pears, he gave the bigger pear to his older brother. Kong Rong, although in Cao Cao's camp, never demonstrated much confidence in or loyalty to Cao Cao. For example, he thought Cao Cao would lose in the Battle of Guandu against the larger forces of Yuan Shao. Kong Rong would mock Cao Cao's promiscuity out of spite when the ruler banned the fermenting of alcohol, a drink which Kong Rong loved, to save on non-essential crop consumption. His behavior would ultimately cost him his life.

emperor, he offended Cao Cao repeatedly and was subsequently put to death. Another early follower of Cao Cao,[10] with a majestic appearance and a moral reputation close to a saint, he was a much-revered figure in society. Cao Cao came up with a far-fetched excuse and forced him to commit suicide. By disposing of its distinguished members, Cao Cao conveyed a clear message to the gentry class — expect no power sharing from me.

Vilified by popular culture, Cao Cao was known to be a tyrant who committed massacres. His worst sin, in the eyes of Confucius critics, was to show disrespect to the emperor by holding him captive. The most famous quote attributed to Cao Cao (which he most likely did not say) was, "Better I betray the whole world than to have the whole world betray me!"[11] How did the devil himself choose his heir? We are about to find out.

CAO CAO CHOOSING HIS SUCCESSOR

Cao Cao allegedly had fifteen consorts and twenty-five sons. His most likely heir should have been his eldest son, adopted by his first wife, who was killed in combat by the surrendered enemy forces. They rebelled because Cao Cao wasted no time after the first truce in having an affair with their leader's aunt.[12] His first wife was naturally furious, having lost her son due to her husband's (historically epic) promiscuity; she left him to lead a life of celibacy.

---

[10] The early follower was Cui Yan (崔琰) who was originally a strategist to Yuan Shao. He joined Cao Cao's camp when Yuan Shao and his sons were defeated one by one. Coming from an aristocratic family and having a great reputation, his actions were scrutinized by Cao Cao. When one of Cui Yan's subordinates wrote a sycophantic piece lauding Cao Cao, Cui Yan, not comfortable with such an attitude, dryly remarked, "Things are never constant." Cao Cao took this as a sign of disloyalty and threw Cui Yan into jail. He was to commit suicide in captivity. Many people lamented his death.

[11] This quote came from a lost ancient book *Za Ji* (雜記), which was written by the ancient Chinese historian Sun Sheng (孫盛) during the Jin dynasty. The quote in its original Chinese is: "宁教我负天下人，休教天下人负我。" See Chen, Shou 陳壽. *San guo zhi* 三國志. Beijing: Zhonghua shuju, 1962, p. 5.

[12] In the battle against Zhang Xiu (张绣), Cao Cao won very swiftly. Zhang Xiu surrendered and Cao Cao laid claim to Zhang Xiu's aunt as well as his troops. Feeling insulted, Zhang Xiu's main advisor Jia Xu (贾诩) told Zhang Xiu that the Cao army had their guard down because the victory was too easy. So Zhang Xiu rearmed his troops and told the Cao army officers that they were to change position in their garrison. Unsuspecting of Zhang's intentions, the Cao army general allowed it. Without a warning signal, the Zhang army attacked the Cao army and the Cao camp was in chaos. In the turmoil, Cao Cao's son Cao Ang and Cao Cao's favorite bodyguard Dian Wei (典韦) were killed.

With his first son dead, Cao Cao's other sons would have the opportunity to become his successor. Cao Cao was particularly fond of his young son whose genius was well illustrated in the following story. When the boy was only six, a warlord gave Cao Cao an elephant as a gift. The people in the court wanted to know the weight of the animal but no scale was large enough to give them a reading. The boy told his father that they could mark the change in the water level by putting the elephant on and off a boat. The weight of the elephant could then be measured by putting rocks of known weight on the boat that would cause the same change in the water level. Bravo! The boy was indeed the Chinese counterpart of Archimedes and his father was extremely impressed.[13] The prodigy, however, fell ill at the age of twelve and died soon after. When one of his sons went to comfort him, Cao Cao said that the death was his great misfortune but a wonderful opportunity for "the rest of you". It was clear that Cao Cao had no intention to follow the traditional way of selecting his successor based on the "eldest son of the main wife" principle. He would choose his heir on the basis of merits, thus providing a level playing field for the princes.

At that time, the frontrunners for the title were the eldest sons Cao Cao had with his main consort, a former geisha who knew how to conduct herself. For example, given her status, she was the first to select gifts for herself from the spoils of victory Cao Cao brought back from the battlefield. The lady, however, never took the most precious items so as not to appear greedy. Neither would she pick the least expensive ones lest others think she was putting on a show. Instead, she always settled for the middle ground. That helped her win the favor of Cao Cao and put her sons in serious contention for the title of crown prince.

The top contenders were the eldest son Cao Pi and third son Cao Zhi. The second son was out of the running early on as, although he was a strong man who could wrestle wild animals with his bare hands and fought alongside his father in

---

[13] The young prince's name was Cao Chong (曹冲). Not only was the young boy a prodigy, he also had a kind heart. In one instance, his father's saddle was chewed by rodents and the attendants, fearing that they would be severely punished, were about to turn themselves in in the hope of receiving a lighter sentence. Cao Chong knew about the situation and told them to wait a while first. Cao Chong then cut little holes in his clothes and pretended to be sad in front of his father as he explained that clothes eaten up by rodents meant bad luck. Cao Cao, comforting his son, told Cao Chong that it was merely a superstition. Cao Chong then told the attendants to tell Cao Cao of the saddle's situation. Cao Cao laughed off the issue stating that even the clothes that were worn by Cao Chong could be chewed, let alone the saddle that had been put in storage.

battles, he lacked political skills. Cao Cao wrote him off at the start of his selection process.

By now it should be clear that Cao Cao cared most about talent when choosing his heir. Particularly close to his heart was literary talent. A gifted poet himself, he valued the same skill set in others. The first prince Cao Pi, an amazing swordsman, was a poet of some renown, having created the seven-character-per-line genre in Chinese poetry. But the family star was the third prince Cao Zhi whose way with words shined more brightly than almost everyone else in Chinese history.[14] Like him, his father Cao Cao and brother the first prince were also regarded among the seven great poets of the period. Yet there had never been any question as to who the most talented member of the Cao family was.

It was therefore only natural that the proud father Cao Cao had thought about making this literary giant his heir. However, as a major poet and a certified genius, the third prince seemed to have granted himself the permission to get drunk. To make things worse, he often messed up when he had one drink too many. On one such occasion, the young prince had his chariot ride through a pathway in the palace reserved for the use of his father, Cao Cao was furious and ordered the execution of the chariot driver.

Furthermore, there was the problem of his inner circle. The third prince's wife was a lady with expensive tastes and liked to flaunt her appetite for luxury in front of others. This deeply offended the militantly frugal Cao Cao who would eventually have his daughter-in-law executed.[15] This reflected badly on the third prince — how was one expected to run a country if he could not even run his own household? It also demonstrated Cao Cao's will to rein in the influence of the gentry class and outer relatives.

---

[14] Xie Lingyun (谢灵运), a famous literary man who lived about 200 years after Cao Cao's time in "the Wei-Jin and Northern and Southern Dynasties" era commented that if all the poetic talents were to fit in one Dan (石), the third prince Cao Zhi's share would be eight Dou (斗) (ten Dou makes one Dan), Xie Lingyun himself would make up one Dou and the sum of all the other poets in all eras would make up the remaining one Dou. Therefore, according to Xie Lingyun, the third prince Cao Zhi represented 80% of the literary talent up to that point. *Cai Gao Ba Dou* (才高八斗) meaning "talent up to eight Dou" is a phrase used in Chinese today to describe anyone with immense scholastic prowess.

[15] Cao Zhi's wife was the niece of the great nobleman Cui Yan who was forced to commit suicide by Cao Cao. Madam Cui's execution could also reflect on Cao Cao's will to minimize the influence of the gentry class, especially the possibility of a member from a key family building a strong outer relative faction in his regime.

Birds of a feather flock together. The third prince's key advisers and close allies were often brilliant individuals whose flamboyance and arrogant display of intelligence would prove to be their undoing. Cao Cao, in selecting his successor, would from time to time subject his two sons to oral examinations. The third prince's key adviser, with his intelligence, was often able to predict the questions that Cao Cao would have for his master.

One of the third prince's key supporters[16] was a gentleman whose talents left even Cao Cao awestruck. Cao Cao had wanted to marry one of his daughters to him but the first prince had said that it was a bad idea because he was blind in one eye. Resentful of the first prince's comment, the one-eyed man became a staunch supporter of the third prince and would speak highly of the talented young man in front of his father. In fact, Cao Cao held the one-eyed man in such high regard that he said he would have married his daughter to him even if he was completely blind.

Then there was another man who was too clever for his own good.[17] Like his master the third prince, he could not help but demonstrate his intelligence whenever the opportunity arose. Perhaps his self-confidence was inherited. He came from a prominent family and had a distinguished pedigree. His ancestor in Western Han was the son-in-law of the author of the monumental *Records of the Grand Historian*. His father was the top military official in Eastern Han and his uncle had been a major warlord before losing to Cao Cao. This noble and intelligent person, a key supporter of the third prince, was a witty person whose urge to shine was so strong that it sometimes clouded his judgment.

Once Cao Cao had a box of desserts and he wrote on the box "A box of pastry" (一合酥). Reading the phrase vertically, one could split the middle character "合" into three words (人一口) and the phrase would read "Each person should have a bite of this pastry" (一人一口酥). Claiming that he was merely following his father's orders, the intelligent nobleman made the third prince finish off the dessert along with a fair amount of alcohol. Cao Cao, a man who liked to make literary jokes himself, laughed it off.

On another occasion, Cao Cao saw the frame of a door to be installed and he wrote the character "to live" (活) on it. The intelligent nobleman saw it and instructed the builders to make the door narrower as "to live" (活) inside the

---

[16] His name was Ding Yi (丁仪), and his father was the governor of the capital in the Eastern Han period and a friend of Cao Cao's.

[17] The man's name was Yang Xiu (杨修). Four of his direct ancestors were commanders of the armed forces in the Eastern Han Dynasty.

"door" (门) in Chinese means "wide" (阔). Apparently, the nobleman considered himself to be so clever that he could read Cao Cao's mind. Cao Cao found his wit to be entertaining up to this point. But as the intelligent nobleman and his master the third prince would soon find out, trying to read the mind of Cao Cao was like playing with fire, especially when it came to matters as important as regime succession.

Cao Cao, in selecting his successor, would subject his two sons to oral examinations. The nobleman, with his intelligence, was always able to correctly guess the topics of these tests. Prior to the interview, he would share his thoughts on these topics with the third prince. As a result, the third prince's performance in these oral examinations were so preternaturally good that they aroused the suspicion of Cao Cao, who soon found out about the nobleman's involvement. Should he make the third prince his heir, Cao Cao reckoned, the nobleman, with his intellect and family background, would surely pose a threat to the descendants and regime of the Cao clan.

Cao Cao, fearing his sons would create factions in court, barred regional officials from meeting with the princes at the capital. Once, the first prince arranged to have his advisor, who had been sent away from the capital,[18] hidden inside a cart and transported to his residence to discuss tactics to win in the succession race. The intelligent nobleman got wind of this and informed Cao Cao. The first prince's advisor, ever the sly thinker, told his panicked master not to worry. He asked the first prince to send a large cart to his own residence and the prince agreed. The next day when the cart arrived, the guards were instructed to check its contents. Lo and behold, the first prince's advisor was not in there. This completely discredited the intelligent nobleman.

It was what happened during one of Cao Cao's last campaigns[19] that turned out to be the final nail in the intelligent nobleman's coffin. With little success on the battlefield, Cao Cao had thoughts to return to the capital. One evening while Cao Cao was having chicken for dinner, he issued a military order: chicken rib. The intelligent nobleman, who had followed Cao Cao to the frontlines, heard the order and started packing. Others on the staff were puzzled and the intelligent

---

[18] The first prince Cao Pi's advisor was Wu Zhi (吴质) who, unlike most of the characters we read in this chapter, came from a lowly family background. He became close to the first prince Cao Pi because of his talent but history would vilify him, most likely because of his birth status.

[19] Cao Cao made a final attempt to unify the country; this time, his target was Liu Bei in the southwest. The campaign was ultimately unsuccessful and he had to live with the fact that he could never unite the country.

nobleman remarked, "Chicken ribs: it is a shame to throw it away but then it is tasteless. Master Cao does not have appetite to continue this war." At that point, Cao Cao decided he had had enough of this aristocratic know-it-all. With his strong gentry background and conspicuous intellect, the intelligent nobleman would be a threat to Cao Cao's regime, especially if he was to make the third prince his heir. Cao Cao accused the nobleman of spreading rumors by misinterpreting his military order and had him executed. From then on, the third prince lost a major source of support.

Unlike his younger brother, the first prince had a much more subdued personality and knew how to conceal his thoughts. His inner circle also exhibited these traits. This turned out to have a decisive influence on the outcome of the succession race. On one occasion when Cao Cao was about to go to battle and key members of the court were present to see him off, the third prince, in his typical flamboyant manner, recited a sublimely beautiful poem that he had written to recount his father's achievements and greatness. This would have been an impossible act to follow for the first prince, whose literary talent was no match for his brother's. But the first prince, following the words of his advisor,[20] lamented that he was worried for his father's safety and cried with a great amount of anguish. The scene was so moving that even Cao Cao shed tears and the ones present all agreed that while the third prince used this opportunity to show off his talents, the first prince was truly filially pious.

Another of the first prince's key supporters was dubbed "the most toxic of strategists in the Three Kingdoms Period" and was directly responsible for killing Cao Cao's eldest son in the military campaign.[21] He had since joined Cao Cao's camp and became one of his most trusted strategists towards the end of the ruler's life. This demonstrated both the strategist's ability and Cao Cao's determination to use the best talent available to him.

Cao Cao, still undecided between the less talented but more stable eldest son and the brilliant but volatile third son, asked the toxic strategist for advice. The advisor, looking up at the ceiling, did not reply. Cao Cao, not used to people not answering him, asked again. The strategist apologized and said he was dwelling

---

[20] The advisor in this instance was Wu Zhi again.

[21] It was Jia Xu who launched a surprise attack on Cao Cao and killed his eldest son Cao Ang in the process. He convinced his then master Zhang Xiu to surrender to Cao Cao and he would eventually become the top military official of the empire.

on the sudden demise of the families of the two Cao Cao's rival warlords[22] who had made the fatal mistake of giving their power to their younger sons. Cao Cao took the hint immediately and the scales were tipped: the first prince was to be his heir.

Nevertheless, Cao Cao did not give up on his third son and gave him another opportunity to prove himself. In a military campaign, Cao Cao instructed the third prince to lead a relief force to the rescue of an embattled general[23] in the hope that the task would instill some sense of responsibility into the great poet. However, Cao Zhi had been so drunk the previous evening that he could not wake up to join the forces the next morning. From then on, Cao Cao lost all hope for the third prince and the first prince Cao Pi's position as the heir was secure. When Cao Cao died, the first prince took over his father's dominions relatively smoothly and he soon deposed the puppet Han emperor, making himself the founding emperor of the Wei Dynasty.

Though he lost in the succession war, the third prince continued to have influence at court and his talents remained a source of jealousy in his relationship with the now emperor Cao Pi.

The following story, whose historical veracity is in doubt, vividly portrays the emotions of love and hate between the brothers.

Still holding a grudge after ascending to the throne, Emperor Cao Pi used a farfetched excuse to accuse his younger brother of treason. He summoned the third prince to the capital and told him at a court meeting that if he could complete a poem on a given topic by literally taking just seven steps, his life would be spared. The topic was "brotherhood" and the rule was that the word "brother" could not be used in the poem. Though in a panic, the third prince Cao Zhi still had a nose as sharp as his mind. He smelled the cooking of beans as he started pacing forward. Then without taking one step more, he recited these words that would provide the gold standard by which all poems on brotherhood and sibling rivalry are measured:

---

[22] Both Yuan Shao, the northern warlord in modern day Hebei province, and Liu Biao (刘表), the southern warlord in modern day Hubei province, gave their domains to their younger sons. This greatly destabilized their families' hold on power in their regions which led to internal rivalries after their death. Cao Cao would take advantage of both of those opportunities and moved to consolidate their areas under his rule.

[23] Cao Cao's cousin and leading general Cao Ren (曹仁) was besieged at the fortress at Fancheng (樊城) by Liu Bei's key general Guan Yu (关羽).

"You burn beanstalk to make fire to fry the beans,
As the beanstalk burns, the beans are crying in the pan;
Are they all not from the root?
Why fry the other in such a hurry?"[24]

Awash in guilt and shame, Emperor Cao Pi let his younger brother return to his granted lands. While this story may be more legend than fact, the third prince Cao Zhi, though sidelined by his brother, did survive Cao Pi and continued to live in relative peace till his death.

ANALYSIS

In Chapter Three of *The Art of War*, Sun Tzu writes: "Attaining one hundred victories in one hundred battles is not the pinnacle of excellence. Subjugating the enemy's army without fighting is." This was how the first prince Cao Pi won the succession race over his much more talented brother, the third prince Cao Zhi.

The third prince was a literary genius and a major poet. This had to mean something to his father Cao Cao whose literary talent was well-documented in history. If he had a head start, his older brother the first prince made up for lost ground by finding a way to his father's heart. He did not try to outshine his younger brother, which would have been impossible. Instead, he quietly built his power base and strengthened his network of support. He had the support of people on his side who knew what made Cao Cao tick and how his mind worked. The most toxic strategist of the Three Kingdoms Period never mentioned the first prince when Cao Cao asked for his recommendation but spoke in such a way that made the father ruler think that choosing his eldest son as heir would best serve the long-term interest of the family.

The third prince's flamboyant personality and tendency to show off turned out to be his greatest liability. This had everything to do with the family dynamics of the imperial court. The king father, as the alpha male, recognized talent and

---

[24] There are two versions of the poem with roughly the same meaning. The older version is as follows:
煮豆持作羹，漉豉以為汁。
萁在釜下燃，豆在釜中泣。
本是同根生，相煎何太急。
The newer version is as such:
煮豆燃豆萁，豆在釜中泣。
本是同根生，相煎何太急？

appreciated abilities. But when talent and abilities asserted themselves too aggressively, they would be perceived as threats by a ruler who had to maintain a firm grip on power at all times. Worse still, when the third prince failed to impose control and discipline upon his own people, like his closest confidante and wife, the ruler father would naturally cast doubts on his ability to lord over the kingdom that the crown prince would inherit. Last but definitely not least, one should not underestimate the emotional needs of an aging father, no matter how much power he still holds. If one could pinpoint a moment in which Cao Cao decided the first prince deserved the throne more than his younger brother, it was when his two sons saw him off for battle. One gave him his immense, unmatched talents. The other gave him his heart. Seen in such a light, the first prince truly subjugated his enemy brother without fighting (trying to match his literary genius). That was the pinnacle of excellence.

Cao Cao's process of selecting his heir was more dangerous than he seemed to realize. He did not adhere strictly to the system of naming the eldest son of the main wife as the heir but instead was partial to the meritocratic system. It had been his original plan to make his favorite prodigy son the heir, but the plan was ruined by the young prince's premature death. He then made public his intentions to let the first prince and third prince compete for the position. Cao Cao's demonstration of indecisiveness caused turmoil in his court and put the life of the loser of the succession race in jeopardy.

CHAPTER 6

Second Prince Li Shimin

Li Yuan
(Founder of Tang Dynasty)

Li Jiancheng
(First Prince/Crown Prince)

Li Yuanji
(Fourth Prince)

LI SHIMIN
(Second Prince/
Emperor Of Tang)

Chapter 4

Brother Against Brothers: Li Shimin's Bloody Ascent to the Top

Dynasty: Tang Dynasty (唐)

Period: circa 610 AD to 630 AD

Key Players:

Tang Gaozu Li Yuan (唐高祖李渊): Founding Emperor of the Tang Dynasty with the title Tang Gaozu (唐高祖)

Li Jiancheng (李建成): Eldest son of Li Yuan, Crown Prince

Tang Taizong Li Shimin (唐太宗李世民): Second son of Li Yuan, later Emperor of Tang with the title Tang Taizong (唐太宗)

Li Yuanji (李元吉): Fourth son of Li Yuan, main supporter of the Crown Prince

"It is the nature of the army to stress speed; to take advantage of the enemy's absence; to travel unanticipated roads; and to attack when they are not alert."

The Art of War, Chapter 11

《兵之情主速，乘人之不及，由不虞之道，攻其所不戒也。》

孙子兵法第十一章

HISTORICAL CONTEXT

China was in constant disarray after the outbreak of the "Yellow Turban Rebellion" in the late second century till the mighty Tang Dynasty was established in the early seventh century.[1] It ushered in arguably the most glorious period in the history of Imperial China.

---

[1] Before Tang, the tumultuous period in Chinese history was known as "the Wei-Jin and Northern and Southern Dynasties" (魏晋南北). The Southern Dynasties were founded by the original noblemen from Northern China while the Northern Dynasties were created by nomads from the Mongolian Steppes. The country was later united by the short-lived Sui Dynasty (隋). Both the Yang (杨) family of the Sui (隋) and the Li (李) family of the Tang (唐) Dynasties came from the Han bloodline but were also related to the nobles of Northern Wei (北魏), Western Wei (西魏) and Northern Zhou (北周). These regimes were founded by tribes from the Mongolian steppes who retained their nomadic traits even after they had entered into the agriculture-based area of northern Han China. They were less compelled to follow the Zhou succession system (see Appendix 1 for further elaboration) and all princes were allowed to participate in military affairs. Women were also given more freedom to express themselves and pursue their goals in life. The legendary female warrior Mulan, for example, allegedly burst onto the scene during this period. The Northern Wei regime united northern China after a period of chaos in 439 AD, though the regime would soon descend into chaos.

When Yuwen Tai (宇文泰), a general in the north, founded Western Wei (西魏) in modern Shaanxi (陕西) and Gansu (甘肃) in 534 AD, he combined his core supporters with the Han Chinese leaders of the area to create a new noble class known as "The Guanlong Aristocracy" (关龙贵族), with the Yang and Li families as its core members. A regime change took place in 557 AD when the Yuwen family replaced Western Wei with the North Zhou Dynasty (北周) which Yang Jian (杨坚), of the Yang family, overthrew in 580 AD. Nine years later, Yang Jian united China under his Sui dynasty. But the triumphs of Yang Jian would soon be eclipsed by a fellow Guanlong aristocrat Li Yuan, who founded the Tang Dynasty after toppling the Sui empire in 618 AD. It is important to note that both Li Yuan's father Li Bing (李昞) and Yang Jian married sisters from the Dugu family

The founder of the Tang Dynasty Li Yuan was a member of the noble class[2] and had three sons with his aristocratic wife.[3] The eldest was Li Jiancheng and the second one, nine years younger than his older brother, was Li Shimin. The fourth son (the third one having died at a young age) was Li Yuanji, who was fourteen years younger than his oldest brother. Li Yuan, as a senior official, had to travel often and he did so usually with his second son Li Shimin. The eldest son Li Jiancheng would stay at home and take care of the Li household along with his younger brother Li Yuanji. This created a strong bond between the two brothers and the resulting family dynamic would have serious implications for the succession battle.

By the time the previous dynasty had fallen into chaos,[4] Li Yuan, a regional official, received an imperial order to defend his jurisdiction against the rebels. Li Yuan's second son Li Shimin, nineteen at the time, convinced his father that since the regime was on its last legs, taking advantage of its decline would be more fruitful than trying to reverse it. Li Yuan then led his troops to take control of the capital, declared himself the new emperor and called his regime Tang. He named his eldest son Li Jiancheng as the crown prince. As China at that time was ruled by warlords scattered all over the country, he ordered the second prince Li Shimin to fight in the west and the fourth prince Li Yuanji to fight in the east.[5] If each of his sons would perform his own function, Li Yuan hoped, a power equilibrium among the brothers would be established. Moreover, entrusting military power to the brothers gave them an opportunity to unify China for the Li family.

(独孤) who was also from the Guanlong aristocracy. The Guanlong aristocracy was the main political force at the time.

[2] During the Sui Dynasty, Li Yuan's family was granted the title Duke of Tang (唐国公) and his jurisdiction was Tai Yuan (太原) in modern-day Shanxi (山西).

[3] Li Yuan's main wife Empress Dou (窦皇后) was of noble birth as her mother was a Northern Zhou princess.

[4] By 617 AD, the Sui Dynasty would fall into chaos and the Sui Emperor Sui Yangdi Yang Guang (隋炀帝杨广) would hide himself in the Southeastern corner in Jiangdu (江都) in modern day Jiangsu, away from the political center of Henan (河南) and Shaanxi (陕西).

[5] Li Yuan led his troops from Shanxi (山西) to take over the capital Chang'an (长安), situated in modern day Xian (西安) in Shaanxi (陕西). Since Sui Yangdi himself was in the east, the campaign was relatively smooth. He initially commanded his second son Li Shimin to fight in Gansu (甘肃) to the west of Chang'an and his fourth son Li Yuanji to fight in Shanxi which was to the east of Chang'an.

Li Yuan's designs, however, were thwarted by the repeated failures of the fourth prince's campaigns in the east which contrasted sharply with the continued success of the second prince's campaigns in the west. This left Li Yuan with little choice but to put his second son in charge of the war effort in the east as well. The second prince had the courage of Alexander the Great when it came to fighting in battles. He would usually bring along fifty or so cavalry soldiers and storm into the enemy camp. This proved to work equally well as a tactic to terrorize the enemy as well as a means to boost the morale of his soldiers.

Having wrested control of the territories from most of the warlords, the second prince played a pivotal role in Tang's unification of China.[6] While his success earned him the loyalty of the military class, it also sowed the seeds of ambition, distrust, and rivalry within the royal family that would have murderous consequences.

THE SECOND PRINCE UPSETTING THE POWER EQUILIBRIUM

The second prince's triumphant return to the capital after unifying China upstaged the Crown Prince and upset the carefully calibrated power equilibrium in court. He was a vassal king, "the general with heaven's mandate", and prime minister all rolled into one.[7] Short of making him his heir, the Emperor bestowed upon the second prince the greatest honors at his disposal.

---

[6] Li Shimin played a pivotal role in Tang's unification of China, especially in the decisive Battle of Luoyang (洛阳之战) and Battle of Hulao Guan (虎牢关之战) in modern-day Henan. Existing side by side with Tang were two hostile regimes, Zheng (郑) led by Wang Shichong (王世充) in Henan and Xia (夏) led by Dou Jiande (窦建德) in Hebei (河北). They were the two thorns in Tang's side and Li Shimin decided to remove them one by one. First, with 80,000 troops, he forced Wang Shichong to retreat to Luoyang and laid siege to the city for a year. To Wang's rescue came Dou Jiande who arrived at Luoyang with an army of 100,000 soldiers. The fearless Li Shimin responded by storming into Dou's camp with just fifty men. This surprise attack was followed by a full-scale invasion that subdued the Dou army. This totally demoralized the Zheng army who surrendered shortly. By eliminating Wang and Dou, Tang now ruled over the most populated and prosperous parts of the country. As for the emperors of these two fallen kingdoms, they were both captured and brought to the capital. But while Wang Shichong, who had a reputation for being righteous, was executed, Dou Jiande, who enjoyed no such popularity, was spared. Throughout Chinese imperial history, emperors had always found the moral authority of their political opponents as threatening as their military might.

[7] He was named the vassal king of Qin (秦王) where Chang'an was situated. While vassal kings in the Tang Dynasty did not have complete administrative control over their

The Crown Prince might have been outshone by the second prince Li Shimin, but he was still very much a force to be reckoned with.[8] For one thing, it was his birthright to succeed his father as emperor. For another, he had the support of the loyal and formidable fourth prince who grew up together with him. Unlike the more militant second prince, the Crown Prince was known to be more conciliatory and preferred peaceful solutions to conflict. For instance, when a subordinate of a defeated warlord rose in rebellion,[9] he proposed to adopt an appeasement policy rather than using force, as suggested by the second prince. His policy worked and the rebellion was put down without bloodshed.

Moreover, having spent years in the capital assisting his father to run the country, the Crown Prince had firmly established his presence and interests in the government. He even extended his influence into the inner court by bribing his father's concubines to speak ill of the second prince.

As the ancient Chinese saying goes, "As there cannot be two suns in the sky, the people cannot have two masters." In the early Tang period, the Emperor, the Crown Prince, and the second prince were all independent centers of power.[10] Bringing the disequilibrium close to a breaking point was the fact that the second prince had the most distinguished generals in his pocket. They had fought under the command of the second prince for years and would only obey orders from their former field marshal.

---

domains, this nonetheless reflected Li Shimin's influence in the most important region of the empire. He was named *Tian Ce Shang Jiang* (天策上将) meaning the "the general with heaven's mandate" and also *Shang Shu Ling* (尚书令) meaning "the prime minister to carry out government policies".

[8] Li Yuan had followed the Zhou succession system (see Appendix 1 for further elaboration) and made Li Jiancheng the crown prince. That was the lesson he learned from history. What led to the rapid demise of the Sui Dynasty, he believed, was the decision of Sui Wendi Yang Jian (隋文帝杨坚) to replace the original crown prince Yang Yong (杨勇) with the infamous Sui Yangdi Yang Guang (隋炀帝杨广) who was responsible for his empire's demise. Li Yuan was therefore adamant to keep the Zhou order in place so as to ensure his dynasty's longevity.

[9] After Li Shimin defeated Dou Jiande (窦建德), Dou's subordinate Liu Heida (刘黑达) rebelled against the Tang regime from their home ground of Hebei (河北).

[10] One case illustrated the administrative chaos at the time: A Li royal family member Li Shentong (李神通) desired a piece of prime real estate which Li Shimin duly allocated to him. Not long after, a concubine asked for the same land from the Emperor Li Yuan, to which the bureaucracy responded that Li Shimin had already given it out to someone else.

The competition between the father and sons became so intense that it spilled over into the conflict between government officials. One of the senior officials[11] who helped the Li family overthrow the previous dynasty was also partial to the second prince. The official expressed his discontent that his honors were less than that of his political rival[12] who himself was loyal to the Emperor. His opponent then used the opportunity to frame the official for treason. The disgruntled official was duly executed by the Emperor Li Yuan, whose intention was most likely to weaken the second prince's influence in the ministerial ranks.

SECOND PRINCE LI SHIMIN'S SHOT TO BE NAMED THE CROWN PRINCE

The conflict between the Crown Prince and the second prince would soon surface in a curious coup d'état. An imperial guard loyal to the Crown Prince[13] staged a rebellion after receiving armor from his master. In an intense, hypersensitive political environment like the Tang Dynasty, princes and leaders of the military force in the capital were usually not allowed to communicate with each other. By sending armor to the guard, therefore, the Crown Prince had broken the law and he was put under house arrest by his suspicious father Li Yuan.[14] The Emperor then ordered the second prince to put down the rebellion and promised him that, should he succeed, he would be named the heir to the throne.

The second prince accomplished his mission, but the Emperor did not keep his end of the bargain by removing the Crown Prince from his position. Even more surprisingly, among the people he held responsible and punished for the revolt, there were two men who worked for the Crown Prince and one who worked for the second prince.[15] Why the sudden turn of events? Why did Li Yuan change his mind? It is impossible to know, for the authoritative history books of

---

[11] The official's name was Liu Wenjing (刘文静).

[12] Liu Wenjing's political rival was called Pei Ji (裴寂).

[13] The guard's name was Yang Wengan (杨文干) and his rebellion happened in 624 AD.

[14] The Emperor Li Yuan naturally was concerned and sent Yuwen Ying (宇文颖) to appease Yang Wengan. Soon Yang Wengan revolted in the name of the Crown Prince along with Yuwen Ying. It was said that Yuwen Ying was on good terms with fourth prince Li Yuanji. Could it have been Li Yuanji's way of forcing Yang Wengan to revolt so as to push the Crown Prince Li Jiancheng to the throne?

[15] This man, called Du Yan (杜淹), was banished by the Emperor to Sichuan (四川) and the second prince Li Shimin, either out of pity or guilt, gave Du Yan 300 taels of gold as compensation.

the period[16] had pitifully little to say about this important incident. One thing, though, was clear. The Emperor did not want any drastic change to the imperial order. He might have also been suspicious of the second prince's involvement.[17] With his designs on the throne exposed, the second prince knew he had to take matters into his own hands.

THE FINAL SHOWDOWN

Eager to maintain the status quo, the Emperor tried to clip the wings of the second prince by sending his most trusted advisers away from the capital.[18] Feeling a sense of encroachment, his people[19] urged their leader to act before it was too late. Imperial succession was a high-stakes game that meted out incredible rewards for the winners and terrible punishments for the losers. No one in the second prince's camp wanted to be losers.

The stage was thus set for the final showdown.[20] With perhaps fortuitous timing, a nationwide drought led to bad harvests and peasant discontent all over the country, often a prelude to regime change in Chinese history. As the sixth month of the year began, events started to unfold and the fate of the three princes as well as the course of history would be changed irrevocably.

FIRST DAY OF THE SIXTH MONTH

Venus appeared in the sky during the day which was, according to astrological calculation, a sign of imminent regime change. That put the second prince under a cloud of suspicion for he was generally regarded as the most likely contender for the throne.[21] At the same time, the Turks launched an attack from the north.

---

[16] The most authoritative books for the era were *The New Book of Tang* (新唐书) and *Zizhi Tongjian* (资治通鉴).

[17] It could likely have been that the second prince Li Shimin ordered Du Yan to stir up the rebellion committed by Yang Wengan and Yuwen Ying in the name of the supporting the Crown Prince Li Jiancheng so that Li Shimin could put down the revolt and be named the heir.

[18] The advisers' names were Fang Xuanling (房玄龄) and Du Ruhui (杜如晦).

[19] A key member was Zhangsun Wuji (长孙无忌), the older brother of Li Shimin's wife and one who would be immensely important for a long period of Tang history.

[20] This happened two years after the "Yang Wengan Rebellion" in 626 AD.

[21] Since the astrological phenomenon appeared above the capital Chang'an, it meant that the vassal king of the Qin territory would become the ultimate leader. The King of Qin was of course none other than the second prince Li Shimin.

The Crown Prince, hoping to weaken the second prince's military dominance, urged his father to put the fourth prince, his loyal younger brother, in charge of an expedition to fight the invasion. He also suggested that top generals from the second prince's camp should join the expedition under the command of the fourth prince. Not only would this give the fourth prince an opportunity to build his military credentials, but it would also draw the second prince's most loyal generals away from him.[22]

SECOND DAY OF THE SIXTH MONTH

On that evening, the second prince was invited to the Crown Prince's palace for a banquet. He alleged that he had thrown up blood after returning to his residence and complained to his father that he must have been poisoned. The Emperor tried to defuse the crisis by blaming it on alcohol and admonishing both the Crown Prince and the second prince.

However, deep down he knew better. Convinced that there was no way for his two sons to get along peacefully under one roof, he toyed with the idea of letting the second prince establish his own domain in the east.[23] He dropped the idea, however, due to the strong objection from the Crown Prince and the fourth prince warning of the danger of civil war, a situation which would be highly unfavorable for them as their second brother was known to be a master in warfare.

THIRD DAY OF THE SIXTH MONTH

Venus was visible in the sky again during the daytime. In the imperial court meeting, the fourth prince was named field marshal to lead the campaign against the Turks with the second prince's top generals under his command. This was clearly a ploy to take power away from the second prince whose strength had

---

[22] According to the *The New Book of Tang* (新唐书) which was written in the Song Dynasty in the 1000s AD, some 400 years after these incidents had happened, fourth prince Li Yuanji was to kill second prince Li Shimin during the ceremony before his journey to fight the Turks. He would then bury all of the generals who were loyal to Li Shimin alive on the way north to the campaign. This was illogical, as how could Li Shimin's generals continue to follow Li Yuanji when their master was murdered before they started the journey?

[23] Emperor Li Yuan suggested that second prince Li Shimin should create his own domain in the East in Louyang (洛阳), an area which Li Shimin conquered for the Tang regime.

become a threat not only to the Crown Prince but to the imperial order. Predictably, the generals refused to go along and urged the second prince to act.[24]

After extended discussions with his people, the second prince finally decided to stage a coup d'état at the capital. He was planning an ambush on the Crown Prince and the fourth prince when he was summoned to the palace by the Emperor. When he saw the Emperor, he told him that the Crown Prince had been having affairs with imperial concubines. In shock, the Emperor demanded to meet with all the princes the next morning. This played into the hands of the second prince who figured that on their way to the Emperor's residence, his rival brothers would have to go through the Northern Gate[25] of the palace. He could have them murdered there as the guard of the gate was loyal to him.[26]

Meanwhile, one of the Emperor's concubines loyal to the Crown Prince[27] overheard the conversation between the Emperor and the second prince and told the Crown Prince about his second brother's accusations. Sensing danger, the fourth prince advised his older brother not to go see the Emperor the next morning. The Crown Prince, however, did not want to act in a way that appeared disrespectful and disloyal to his father. He would go to the meeting the next morning.

FOURTH DAY OF THE SIXTH MONTH

As daylight broke, the Crown Prince and the fourth prince took the shortest route to the palace through the Northern Gate. The guard of the gate asked the Crown Prince to leave his soldiers outside, as he was required to do so when entering the residence of the Emperor. Waiting for the Crown Prince and the fourth prince inside the premises were the second prince and his people.[28] As they entered, the

---

[24] The generals include Yuchi Jingde (尉迟敬德) and Chen Shubao (陈叔宝) who fought alongside with second prince Li Shimin in the wars of unification of China for the Tang Dynasty.

[25] The Northern Gate is known as Xuanwu Men (玄武门) which represents the northern star in traditional Chinese culture. The color that it symbolizes is black and its spirit animal is the turtle or snake.

[26] The guard at the Northern Gate was named Chang He (常何). Chang He was previously a guard at second prince Li Shimin's palace, and the Crown Prince had tried to bribe him via his advisor Wei Zheng. Despite that, Chang He continued to be loyal to Li Shimin.

[27] The concubine's name is Zhang Jieyu (张婕妤).

[28] Second Prince Li Shimin's forces were led by the great generals Yuchi Jingde, Chen Shubao, Cheng Yaojin (程咬金) and Zhang Shigui (张士贵).

fourth prince, an archery master, saw his second brother's entourage and shot an arrow at him. But he missed, not only once but three times, probably due to the fact that he was facing east, and the sun was shining in his face. The Crown Prince was thus shot to death by his second brother.

The fighting that followed must have been chaotic as the second prince, a seasoned horseman, fell from his horse. As the fourth prince went over to his brother and tried to strangle him with his bow, he was stopped and killed by one of the second prince's soldiers. The second prince's generals then led their men[29] to the inner palace and told the Emperor that the Crown Prince and the fourth prince had staged a coup but thanks to the second prince, order was now restored.

The Emperor Li Yuan, effectively held captive, handed administrative power over to the second prince. He, having achieved total victory over his brothers, went to their residences and killed all their sons, including a toddler. Any potential threat had to be eliminated and therefore no prisoners would be taken, not even one's innocent nephews. Lest there be any doubt that he was now the de facto ruler, the second prince took one of the fourth prince's concubines as his own. The shocked and melancholic Emperor abdicated soon after. He was to assume the powerless role of "Supreme Emperor"[30] and led a life of almost total seclusion till his death nine years later.

Li Shimin, having murdered his brothers and with blood on his hands, attempted to tamper with history. As required by law, the histories of the emperor were to be recorded by scribes. The emperor was not supposed to have access to these records. Li Shimin, however, asked to read what was written about him three times. The scribes said no to him twice but capitulated eventually. The question is, once Li Shimin was given access to these records, did he tamper with them?

It is not only possible but likely, judging by how harshly his brothers were portrayed in the history books. For example, the former Crown Prince Li Jiancheng was presented as a womanizing alcoholic who only cared for hunting. Perhaps not accidentally, these were the exact traits Confucian scholars found most abominable. Another interesting case was the general who guarded the Northern Gate[31] and played a key role in Li Shimin's coup d'état. No account of his life was ever given in any official histories. Only the biography on his tombstone, which was later discovered, shed light on his life. Having risked his life by

---

[29] Yuchi Jingde was the leader for that operation.

[30] The term for "Supreme Emperor" is *Taishang Huang* (太上皇).

[31] Chang He (常何).

taking part in the most sinister of plots, he was rewarded handsomely in financial terms by Li Shimin, though he was never promoted to higher positions.

Regardless of how he rose to the apex of power, Li Shimin was to become one of the most successful emperors in imperial Chinese history presiding over a glorious period in the Tang Dynasty.[32] During his reign, the Tang Empire defeated the Eastern Turks and its influence reached deep into Central Asia. Also, culturally, the Tang Empire was viewed as the center of civilization by neighbors such as Japan and Korea. Confucianism likes to correlate moral character with worldly success. But in this case as in many others, this is not borne out in history.

ANALYSIS

"The key factor to winning is speed: to take advantage of the enemy's unprepared-ness and attack via an unanticipated path so as to strike where he is least fortified."

The Art of War, Chapter 11

This summarizes the manner in which the second prince seized the Tang throne. Emperor Li Yuan, his father, was weak and indecisive compared to his more formidable sons, the Crown Prince and the second prince. As a result, the players of the succession game had to take matters in their own hands rather than wait and let their father make up his mind.

As we have seen, when the situation became urgent and required him to act, the second prince attacked at full speed and with maximum power. After all, he had substantially more military experience and successes than his two brothers. *The Art of War* discusses at length the use of spies and its importance to military success. The second prince apparently understood this very well. By buying off the head guard at the Northern Gate, he turned his brothers into prey wandering haplessly into the hunting ground.

What happened to the Li royal family was a tragedy of Shakespearean dimensions. This could be attributed to the power disequilibrium that existed between the Emperor, the Crown Prince, and the second prince. As Emperor Li Yuan sought to build his empire, he relied on his sons who were more trustworthy than people outside of the family. This was also in line with the nomadic tradition

---

[32]The period was known as Zhenguan Zhizhi (贞观之治) (626–649 AD), named after the imperial era of Li Shimin.

of the Li family that involved all males of the household in hunting. It was the Emperor's plan to make his sons the three legs of the tripod that supported the Tang Empire.

The tripod lost one of its legs when the fourth prince's campaign went awry. The second prince took over the eastern battle front and went on to become the undisputed field marshal who unified China under the Tang Dynasty. His military accomplishments were simply too great to be ignored. However, there was no legal or political basis for replacing the Crown Prince. When the Emperor let his princes get involved in state affairs, they would inevitably attract supporters and competing factions would form. As the center could not hold, all parties, knowingly or not, were bracing for a showdown. Since their fates and fortunes became inextricably intertwined, supporters would edge their masters ever closer to confrontation when they detected signs of their factions losing ground in the succession battle.

This story sheds light on the fundamental dilemma imperial families in ancient China faced between growth and internal power struggle. By letting his sons have a piece of the action, the father encouraged competition and provided training for the ones participating in building the imperial enterprise. But there was a price to pay. Factions would almost certainly develop, leading to a bloody rivalry between siblings. The three sons of Li Yuan were competent, but the power structure forced them to direct their aggression against one another, culminating in the final showdown at the Northern Gate. Interestingly, both the Song (960–1279 AD) and Ming (1368–1644 AD) Dynasties, which came after the Tang, formulated policies to check the participation of princes in politics. While this might be effective in stopping the development of factions and stemming rivalry within the royal court, it also guaranteed that whoever finally ascended to the throne would lack training in competition and aggression. The second prince created one of the most glorious periods in Chinese history. But the truth is he could not have pulled it off without first murdering his brothers.

Ninth Prince Li Zhi

Li Shimin
（Emperor of Tang）

First Prince/
Crown Prince

Fourth
Prince

Originally Consort to

LI ZHI
(Ninth Prince/
Emperor Of Tang)

Wu Zetian

Empress Wang

Chapter 5

Li Zhi: The Tai Chi Master of Court Politics

Dynasty: Tang Dynasty (唐)

Period: circa 640 AD to 700 AD

Key Players:

Tang Taizong Li Shimin (唐太宗李世民)**:** Emperor of Tang with the title Tang Taizong (唐太宗)

Tang Gaozong Li Zhi (唐高宗李治)**:** Ninth son of Li Shimin, later named Crown Prince, then Emperor of Tang with the title Tang Gaozong (唐高宗)

Empress Wang (王皇后)**:** Li Zhi's First Empress, later deposed

Wu Zetian (武则天)**:** Originally Li Shimin's consort, later Li Zhi's Empress, then founder of her dynasty, the only female emperor in Chinese history

"Deception is the essence of human engagement. The competent must show incompetence overtly and the ambitious must demonstrably express his lack of ambition."

The Art of War, Chapter 1
《兵者，诡道也。故能而示之不能，用而示之不用。》
孙子兵法第一章

HISTORICAL CONTEXT

One would think that given his experience, the Emperor Li Shimin (second prince from Chapter 4) would take great pains to create a power equilibrium within his household. But try as he might, he could not prevent his sons from fighting for the throne.

Li Shimin had three sons with his empress: They were the first prince, the fourth prince and the ninth prince Li Zhi.[1] The first prince was named crown prince early on as he was the eldest son. His position seemed secure, but his fortune would fall rapidly after his mother's death[2] as he took one misstep after another. As the first prince approached adulthood, he would develop a few traits which were abominable to his father. Both of his parents had ancestral roots which could be traced to the Siberian tribes and the first prince seemed to have inherited their nomadic traits. A great fan of Turkic culture, he once remarked that there was nothing he wanted more than to become a general of the great Turkic khan. This would be a worthy goal for anyone but the crown prince of the Tang Empire. It gave his emperor father cause for thought about what kind of diplomatic relations the central kingdom would have with its northern rival if his successor was so infatuated with the Turkic way of life. Moreover, the first prince was involved

---

[1] Li Shimin had three sons with his Empress Zhangsun (长孙皇后). The Tang royal family seemed to follow the Zhou succession system of exalting the sons from the main wife (嫡出) and their names could illustrate this point. The name of the oldest son Chengqian (承乾) means to inherit the first and most powerful hexagram from the *I-Ching* "Qian" (乾). The fourth son's name Tai (泰) was also taken from the *I-Ching* (易经) and the Tai hexagram means prosperity. The ninth son was named Zhi (治) which meant to rule. These was of sharp contrast to the third son's name, Ke (恪), which meant to "remain in one's position". Therefore, from the names they were given, one could see who had a chance to inherit the throne.

[2] Empress Zhangsun would meet her premature death in 636 AD at the age of thirty-five.

with a male consort[3] and as soon as his father learned of the affair, the male consort was put to death. This further strained the father and son's relationship.

As the first prince's status was fading in his father's eyes, his fourth brother was gaining in favor. Li Shimin, a first rate general himself, realized he had to rely on Confucian values that prized loyalty above everything else to maintain his rule. He therefore attached great importance to the study of classics, and the fourth prince happened to be a man of great learning. The emperor was so impressed with his son that he bestowed upon him some of the greatest honors that a prince could receive. The first prince felt threatened and got himself involved in a rebellion,[4] emulating his father in a clumsy attempt to take power by force. The rebellion was quickly put down and the first prince was sent into exile.

Later, the first prince was allowed to have a heart-to-heart talk with his father. He told the Emperor that he never meant to do him any harm. He was just trying to act preemptively before the fourth prince could make his move against him. Li Shimin was not entirely convinced but could not help but wonder if his favorite son had a dark side.

THE RISE OF THE NINTH PRINCE

The Emperor's suspicion was further aroused when he spoke with the fourth prince about his plans for the future if he was to become emperor. The fourth prince said when the time came for him to pass the throne, he would name his younger brother the ninth prince Li Zhi as his successor. The Emperor found this hard to believe. The ninth prince meanwhile had a special place in the heart of his father. Not only was he the youngest son from the empress, he had a miserable childhood as his mother died when he was only eight. Therefore, when the timid ninth prince told his father that his fourth brother had threatened to incriminate him as a co-conspirator in the rebellion, it was clear to the Emperor that the fourth prince was a menace to his brothers. If he was to succeed him, Li Shimin's other sons would certainly perish.

Towards the end of Li Shimin's reign, the most powerful official in court was his empress' brother.[5] He decided that, as chancellor, he would rather serve the

---

[3] The male consort was named Chengxin (称心).

[4] The instigator of the revolt was another of Li Shimin's sons, Li You (李祐).

[5] The minister's name was Zhangsun Wuji (长孙无忌). The Zhangsun family was a branch of the royal family of the Northern Wei Dynasty (北魏) (386–534 AD) which was the root

weak and deferential ninth prince than the aggressive and dominant fourth prince. He therefore strongly argued for the ninth prince to be named the new crown prince. The Emperor agreed and the ninth prince Li Zhi was named the heir to the throne.

WU ZETIAN ENTERED THE TANG PALACE

An innocent fourteen-year-old girl, later known by the name Wu Zetian, entered Emperor Li Shimin's inner court as a low-ranking concubine.[6] Her father[7] was a wood merchant who became Tang's minister of infrastructure because of his participation in the founding emperor's uprising that helped topple the previous Dynasty. He had two sons from his first marriage. After the death of his first wife, he married a forty-four-year-old lady who was related to the royal family of the previous dynasty.[8]

Unlike her contemporaries in ancient China, the forty-four-year-old lady was much more into reading history than sewing and knitting. This trait would be inherited by her middle daughter Wu Zetian. When Wu Zetian was twelve, her father passed away. Together with her mother and her sisters, she was left in the care of her half-brothers who did not treat them kindly. This toughened up Wu Zetian who learned how to fend for herself whenever it was necessary. This also hardened her resolve to find a better life away from the Wu clan. Such an opportunity seemed to present itself when teenage girls from noble families were invited to enter the court to be chosen as concubines of the emperor.

---

of the latter regimes of Western Wei (西魏) (535–557 AD), Northern Zhou (北周) (557–581 AD), Sui (隋朝) (581–618 AD), and Tang (唐朝) (618–906 AD) itself. Zhangsun Wuji represented the greatest political force of the time known as "The Guanlong Aristocracy" (关龙贵族) which comprised of the noble families that controlled the key areas of government from the Western Wei onwards. It is important to note that Empress Zhangsun advised Li Shimin against relying on Zhangsun Wuji. The events that were to unfold would demonstrate the wisdom of the young empress.

[6] In the Tang Dynasty, the inner court was organized as the following in order of seniority: there was 1 Empress, 4 Furen(s) (夫人), 9 Pin(s) (嫔), 9 Jieyu(s) (婕妤), 9 Meiren(s) (美人) and 9 Cairen(s) (才人). Wu Zetian entered and remained in the rank of Cairen in the entirety of Li Shimin's reign.

[7] Wu Zetian's father's name was Wu Shiyue (武士彟).

[8] The lady's last name was Yang (杨), which was the imperial surname of the previous Sui Dynasty (隋). She and Wu Shiyue had three daughters together and Wu Zetian was the middle child of the three.

Wu Zetian, upon entering into the Emperor's harem, would remain in that status for as long as Li Shimin lived. This, coupled with the fact that she did not bear the Emperor any children, suggested that the Emperor had never granted her any favor.[9]

As the heir to the throne, the ninth prince was by his father's side most of the time. The Crown Prince performed his filial duties perfectly. When the Emperor had an infection on his leg, for example, he would suck the pus from his father's wound. It was during his time in his father's palace that he came to know Wu Zetian, who was four years his senior.[10] That Wu Zetian was officially his stepmother did not prevent the Crown Prince from having an affair with her in his father's palace. Maybe he was not so filially pious and timid after all.

WU ZETIAN ENTERED AGAIN

When the Emperor died, all his childless concubines including Wu Zetian were sent by royal edict to a Buddhist temple where they were to spend the rest of their lives.[11] On the anniversary of the late emperor's death, Li Zhi, now Emperor of Tang, visited the temple and reunited with his former lover and stepmother. The Emperor at the time had two important women in his life: Empress Wang and his favorite consort. Politically, the Tang Dynasty was dominated by the trans-generational influence of a few major families. One of these families was the Wang family whose daughter had married Li Zhi when he was still a prince.

---

[9] A story may offer some clues on the young Wu Zetian's personality and why Li Shimin may have been wary of her: one day the emperor showed the members of his harem an untamed horse, an insult to a master horseman like himself. When asked what should be done to tame the mighty stallion, Wu Zetian responded that she only needed three things to complete the task: a metal whip, a hammer and a dagger. When asked how she would use these items, she said that she would start with the metal whip. If the horse would not succumb to her wishes, she would hit it with a metal hammer. Finally, she would kill the animal with a dagger if it persisted in disobedience. The rest of the entourage along with the Emperor Li Shimin was naturally shocked by her answer. Wu Zetian's tough personality was clearly demonstrated in the episode.

[10] Perhaps due to his mother's death during his early years, ninth prince Li Zhi had a strong reliance on older and more authoritative women. Li Zhi had a teacher who was the concubine of his grandfather Li Yuan. When Li Zhi became an adult, the teacher wanted to become a Taoist nun. Not able to stand the separation, Li Zhi would build a Taoist temple for his former teacher in the palace so he could see her on a regular basis.

[11] The Buddhist Temple's name was Ganye Si (感业寺).

However, Empress Wang was a proper lady and apparently not Li Zhi's cup of tea, and they did not have any children together. Empress Wang's main rival was the favored consort who was also from a prominent family. Unlike the Empress, however, the favored consort bore the Emperor a son and two daughters.[12]

Since the Emperor's visit to the temple, his relationship with Wu Zetian had become the subject of court gossip. Empress Wang saw a value play here: Wu Zetian could help her break the spell of the favorite consort on the Emperor. Moreover, since Wu Zetian was formerly a concubine to the Emperor's late father, she would never threaten her status as empress. An enemy's enemy could be one's friend. Empress Wang got in touch with Wu Zetian and told her to remain patient and regrow her hair. A year later when Wu Zetian's hair had fully regrown, Empress Wang brought her back to the palace in violation of Confucian rules of familial order, but much to the joy of the Emperor. Wu Zetian, wised up by experience, was determined to make the most of her second chance. She went to great lengths to maintain a good relationship with not only her benefactor Empress Wang but all the court ladies, many of whom she bribed for intelligence.

Within a year of Wu Zetian's return to the palace, she was made a lady-in-court of the second rank.[13] A year later, she bore the Emperor a son[14] while the favored consort had ceased to bear any children since Wu Zetian's return. It dawned on Empress Wang that she had brought in a tiger too fierce for her to control. As her enemy's enemy did not turn out to be her friend, she joined hands with her former rival, the favored consort, and began to speak ill of Wu Zetian in

---

[12]Empress Wang came from an extremely prominent family, the Wangs from Taiyuan (太原) in modern day Shanxi (山西). The Tang Dynasty was still operated by and large like "the Wei-Jin and Northern and Southern Dynasties" (魏晋南北) (220–580 AD) where the regime was dominated by a trans-generational influence of the major families. Even the Li royal family had to build relations with these families and hence Li Zhi, the Crown Prince, was married to a daughter from the Taiyuan Wang family. Empress Wang's main rival was the much-loved Consort Xiaoshu Fei (萧淑妃) who was also from the prominent royal family of the Qi (479–502 AD) (齐) and Liang (502–557 AD) (梁) regimes in the Southern Dynasties (南朝). Li Zhi and Xiaoshu Fei had a son and two daughters together and Li Zhi made their son the vassal king of Yong (雍), an area that covered the capital Chang'an (长安) in modern day Shaanxi (陕西). This was a higher title than what was normally bestowed to sons from consorts because the vassal area was the center of imperial power. Xiaoshu Fei therefore had a strong position in her rivalry with the Empress Wang.

[13]Wu Zetian was named one of the Furen(s) (夫人) with the title Zhaoyi (昭仪).

[14]Li Zhi and Wu Zetian's eldest son was named Li Hong (李弘).

front of the Emperor. In retaliation, Wu Zetian gave her rivals a dose of their own medicine whenever possible. The Emperor tried to remain impartial and allowed the drama to unfold naturally.

WU ZETIAN AS EMPRESS

The power equilibrium that Emperor Li Zhi tried to maintain was drastically upset when Wu Zetian's infant daughter died under dubious circumstances just moments after Empress Wang's visit. Some historical accounts hinted at Wu Zetian murdering her own daughter in order to frame Empress Wang while others maintained that she was innocent.[15] Whether this is fact or fiction is a matter of opinion. But, at the end of the day, only the opinion of one man mattered: The Emperor. He chose to believe in Wu Zetian, or so it seemed. Li Zhi wanted to strip Empress Wang of her title, but the two main chancellors vehemently opposed the idea.[16]

Li Zhi would have brushed aside the objections if they had been raised by anyone other than the two. When the twenty-one-year-old Li Zhi was made Emperor, his father Li Shimin appointed the two chancellors as minister regents, which was tantamount to giving them the guardianship of the young ruler. Undeterred, Wu Zetian decided to go on the offensive. When a court lady found inside Wang's chambers a small doll with Wu Zetian's name and date of birth written on it, she accused the Empress and her mother of performing sorcery on her. Given the difficulty in assessing evidence and verifying details, accusing someone of sorcery had always been a low-cost, convenient way to smear one's

---

[15] According to *The Old Book of Tang* (旧唐书), written during "the Five Dynasties and Ten Kingdoms" period (906–960 AD), Empress Wang visited Wu Zetian's daughter and the infant princess died shortly after. Wu Zetian then accused Empress Wang of murdering her baby. In later accounts of the *The New Book of Tang* (新唐书) and *Zizhi Tongjian* (资治通鉴) which were written in the Northern Song Dynasty (960–1125 AD), it was Wu Zetian who killed her own daughter after Empress Wang's visit. In other words, to eliminate a political rival, Wu Zetian had committed a crime of unspeakable horror.

[16] The two gentlemen were Zhangsun Wuji (长孙无忌) and Chu Suiliang (褚遂良). Zhangsun Wuji's background was outlined above. As for Chu Suiliang, he was the son of Chu Liang (褚亮), who had been a member of Li Shimin's inner circle before he took the throne. The two belonged to the faction of the aristocrats whose interest would be best served when the imperial authority of the Emperor was held in check. That was why they were against deposing Empress Wang, who was from the noble Taiyuan Wang line. The last thing that they wanted was to tip the balance in favor of the emperor.

enemy in the inner court. The Emperor took the accusation seriously enough to block communication between the Empress and her mother.[17] Did he believe Wu Zetian? Not necessarily. He might have been using the rivalry to assert his authority and rein in the influence of the aristocracy.

The showdown between imperial and aristocratic authorities took place when the Emperor met with his two ministers to discuss deposing Empress Wang. The ministers reminded the Emperor that the Empress had been chosen by his father Li Shimin. Given her family background and the lack of evidence to substantiate Wu Zetian's accusation, there was no basis for her deposal. Then one of the ministers spoke the unspeakable: Wu Zetian was the late emperor's concubine; how could the Emperor make his stepmother his empress? As he spoke, the minister repeatedly kowtowed on the floor and his forehead started bleeding. At that point, a female voice from behind the curtain said, "Why not beat the old man to death?" It was Wu Zetian. The ministers of the cabinet remained adamant and signed a petition against making Wu Zetian the empress.

Conspicuously absent from the meeting was the third minister regent[18] who was a top general trusted by the late emperor Li Shimin. The old military man met with the Emperor in private and stressed that the choice of empress was a personal decision for the Emperor to make alone. There were other senior officials who saw this as an opportunity to pit the Emperor against the top two minister regents.[19] Somewhat paradoxically, the Minister of Manners and Morals[20] was one of those in favor of deposing the Empress. A pro-Wu Zetian faction soon developed in court. Eventually the will of the Emperor prevailed. Not only did he make Wu Zetian the empress, he also removed the two minister regents appointed by his father to keep him in check.

The most senior minister regent, as the Emperor's uncle,[21] was ordered to commit suicide and many of his family members were executed. The other

---

[17] Moreover, the brother of Empress Wang's mother, who was also from the prominent family of Liu (柳氏), was demoted from his ministerial position in the capital to a local government posting.

[18] His name was Li Ji (李勣).

[19] An official named Li Yifu (李义府) was previously sidelined by Zhangsun Wuji and he used the situation to support Li Zhi's appointment of Wu Zetian as Empress. The Chinese idiom "*Xiao Li Cang Dao* (笑里藏刀)" (hiding a dagger inside one's smile) was used to describe Li Yifu. One could only imagine his scheming ways from the idiom that was produced in his honor.

[20] His name was Xu Jingzong (许敬宗).

[21] Zhangsun Wuji.

minister regent[22] was exiled to the south and would eventually perish there. Both Empress Wang and the favored consort[23] were banished to the "cold palace", a small hut inside the palace away from the Emperor. A month after their fall from grace, the Emperor visited and spoke to them via a small hole. Wu Zetian knew about this and ordered their execution with poison.

WU ZETIAN'S RISE IN POWER

Replacing Empress Wang with Wu Zetian as Empress was the master stroke of the Emperor to purge his court of aristocratic influence. The resulting power vacuum was filled by the strong-willed Wu Zetian. The timing was also opportune for this extraordinary woman. The Emperor could have been suffering from high blood pressure which caused him to have severe headaches and affected his eyesight. This gave Wu Zetian the opportunity to take over her husband's duties. For the first time in Chinese history, the Empress met with senior ministers and made decisions on how to run the country. To eradicate any potential threat to her and her offspring, she banished the eldest son that Li Zhi had sired with a concubine away from the capital and had him murdered shortly after.[24] The ascent of Wu Zetian marked the culmination of the steady rise of women in politics from the Northern Wei to the Tang Dynasty whose nomadic origins had resulted in less male-dominated regimes unlike the more traditional Confucian Han, Song, and Ming dynasties.

It was not long before Wu Zetian's authority was perceived as a threat at court. A eunuch, apparently obeying orders from a much higher authority, accused Wu Zetian of performing sorcery. The Emperor, under the influence of his prime minister,[25] granted permission to draft a royal edict to depose Wu Zetian. It did not take long for the eternally vigilant Wu Zetian to find out about this machination against her and she hit back by accusing the minister of treason. Whether voluntarily or otherwise, the Emperor sided with his wife again and executed the minister together with his entire family with the only exception of

---

[22] Chu Suiliang.

[23] Xiaoshu Fei.

[24] The prince's name was Li Zhong (李忠).

[25] The chancellor, Shangguan Yi (上官仪), was one of the first to attain such a high position by beginning his career through the nascent imperial examination system rather than by being of noble birth. This class of bureaucracy would come to dominate politics in the Song Dynasty while at this juncture of Chinese history in the Tang Dynasty, these scholars from examinations would have a long-term rivalry with the men from the aristocracy.

his granddaughter,[26] who, in another strange plot twist in Chinese history, would become a key female minister of Wu Zetian (she would appear in Chapter Six).

It was impossible to know if the Emperor would have stemmed the rise of Wu Zetian if he had been less troubled by his health problems. What was not in doubt was that his illness gave his wife the leverage to accumulate power. Wu Zetian excelled in mind games, and she used the sorcery incident to guilt trip the Emperor into raising her status further. She became the co-ruler of Tang with her husband.[27] At the pinnacle of her power, Wu Zetian went on to show the world what a wise ruler she was. For one thing, she did not infest the court with members of her own family. In fact, she even banished several members of the Wu family to the south. It was not until the end of her husband's life that she began to let her nephews[28] hold government office. While this might have something to do with the fact that she suffered at the hands of the Wu clan after the death of her father, this conveyed an impression of impartiality and gave her moral authority. For another, she knew how to run a country. The population of the Tang Empire doubled during her rule, an important measure of peace and prosperity in an agricultural society.

As the Emperor's health declined, Wu Zetian tightened her grip on the government. Her lust for power poisoned the relationship with her children. Wu Zetian's first son[29] had a soft demeanor like his father. He was talented and was kind enough to try to find husbands for his two older sisters from his father's disgraced consort.[30] He also demanded a burial place for his murdered oldest half-brother.[31] However, he suffered from tuberculosis and died at a young age.[32] Li Zhi and Wu Zetian's second son[33] took after his grandfather Li Shimin more than his father. As what was required of a future ruler, he was a competent general and knowledgeable about history and literature. Following in the footsteps of his grandfather and his fourth uncle, he put together a team of top writers to work on

---

[26] Her name was Shangguan Waner (上官婉儿).

[27] The couple would be known as *Er Sheng* (二圣) meaning "The 2 holies".

[28] One of her staunchest supporters from the Wu clan was her nephew Wu Sansi (武三思).

[29] Li Hong (李弘).

[30] Xiaoshu Fei.

[31] Li Zhong.

[32] *The New Book of Tang* (新唐书), written in the more patriarchal Song Dynasty with a clear motive of smearing Wu Zetian, made the unsubstantiated claim that Li Hong was killed by his own mother.

[33] His name was Li Xian (李贤).

the annotations of the most important historical texts.[34] However, his strong and ambitious personality did not sit well with his equally competitive mother Wu Zetian. Rumor also had it that the second son was the son of Li Zhi and Wu Zetian's sister.[35] The conflict between mother and son came to a head when the witch doctor,[36] who was treating Li Zhi, was killed. Since the witch doctor had spoken ill of the empress' second son, the prince naturally became a prime suspect. Moreover, like his first uncle, the prince had a male consort who had been arrested. What was worse, military equipment was found at the prince's palace, making him appear guilty of plotting a revolt. There was speculation that the prince had to take pre-emptive action to save himself as he was losing favor with his parents. He was put under house arrest and Wu Zetian ordered his execution two years after his father's death.

WU ZETIAN AS EMPEROR

As the Emperor's condition continued to deteriorate, an acupuncturist[37] suggested a treatment that involved inserting pins into his head to let a good amount of blood out. Wu Zetian considered the procedure too dangerous and wanted to have the doctor executed. The Emperor, however, decided that he had little to lose. The procedure turned out to be a success and he had a period of recovery. Wu Zetian was overjoyed and rewarded the physician handsomely. Later accounts of this incident in the history books vilified Wu Zetian by misrepresenting that she had blocked treatment for the Emperor in order to rule the country on her own. The Emperor Li Zhi was often portrayed as weak and ineffectual to serve as the perfect foil to the dominant, power-hungry Wu Zetian. But as his insistence on being treated demonstrated, the Emperor was not as submissive as he was made out to be in the relationship.

When the Emperor Li Zhi died, he passed the throne to his third son[38] with Wu Zetian. But Wu Zetian, the one with all the power, had other plans. She used

---

[34] Under Li Xian's supervision, the team ended up producing the most authoritative annotation for the *The Book of Later Han* (后汉书); still known today by his name as the *Zhanghuai Annotation* (章怀注).

[35] Wu Zetian's sister was Lady Helan (贺兰氏). There might be some truth to it: Li Zhi, true to his imperial nature, also had affairs with Wu Zetian's sister Lady Helan and her daughter when they moved to the palace after Lady Helan became a widow.

[36] His name was Ming Chongyan (明崇俨).

[37] The man's name was Qin Minghe (秦鸣鹤).

[38] He was named Li Zhe (李哲).

various excuses to remove her own sons from power and put to death members of the Li royal family. According to *The Old Book of Tang*, of the 113 unnatural deaths of the Li family members during the Tang Dynasty, seventy perished under Wu Zetian. Having eliminated all political opposition, Wu Zetian proceeded to take the final step to make herself the absolute monarch. She made her fourth son,[39] who had replaced his brother as emperor, abdicate and hand over the throne. Wu Zetian established her own regime named Zhou (周) and became the first (and only) female emperor in Chinese history.

ANALYSIS

"Deception is the essence of human engagement. The competent must show incompetence overtly and the ambitious must demonstrably express his lack of ambition."

The Art of War, Chapter 1

The Emperor Li Zhi was one of the most intriguing characters in Chinese history. In the eyes of many historians, he was a minor player whose ascending to the throne was an accident of history. Had his older and more competent brothers not damaged themselves politically, he would never have been named crown prince. Then he succumbed to his nature to be dominated when he fell for the older and more powerful Wu Zetian. He then died and left his children and his descendants at the mercy of the mighty and vicious Wu Zetian. But the Emperor Li Zhi was so much more than meets the eye. While he did not actively participate in the struggle for the title of crown prince, it was the insinuations he made to his father about what a threat the fourth prince was that effectively put an end to his brother's political career.

Li Zhi's apparent meekness stood in stark contrast to the fourth prince's shining brilliance and overt ambition. This worked to his advantage. For the royal family, what mattered most was peace and domestic harmony which could only be achieved when a power equilibrium was established. A family member of extraordinary abilities and aspirations would upset the balance of power and therefore was often regarded with suspicion, if not treated with downright hostility.

Once in power, Li Zhi proved himself to be a master in manipulating the power relationship between opposite forces. The rivalry between Empress Wang

---

[39] His name was Li Dan (李旦).

and Wu Zetian played right into his hands and he used the opportunity to free himself from the control imposed upon him by his late father through the minister regents and rein in the aristocratic influence in his court. That was akin to killing two birds with one stone. Although he seemed to be dominated by Wu Zetian, one should not lose sight of the role his poor health had played. Towards the end of his life, his decision to go ahead with the acupuncture treatment was a sign that he continued to be in the driver's seat in the relationship.

CHAPTER 4

Third Prince Li Longji

Li Zhi
[Emperor of Tang]

Wu Zetian
[Emperor of Zhou]

Empress
Wei

Li Zhe
[Emperor of Tang]

Li Dan
[Emperor of Tang]

Princess
Taiping

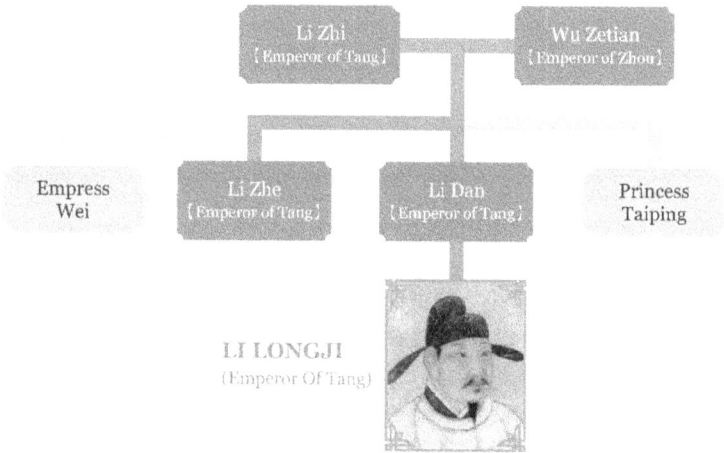

LI LONGJI
(Emperor Of Tang)

Chapter 6

Li Longji: Thriving on Chaos

Dynasty: Tang Dynasty

Period: circa 710 AD to 715 AD

Key Players:

Wu Zetian (武則天): Li Zhi's Empress, then founder of the Zhou Dynasty, the only female emperor in Chinese history

Tang Zhongzong Li Zhe (唐中宗李哲): Third son of Li Zhi and Wu Zetian, became emperor and then deposed by his mother, became emperor again after Wu Zetian lost power with the title Tang Zhongzong (唐中宗)

Empress Wei (韦皇后): Wife of Li Zhe, attempted to emulate her mother-in-law Wu Zetian to become the supreme female leader of the Tang Empire

Tang Ruizong Li Dan (唐睿宗李旦): Fourth son of Li Zhi and Wu Zetian, became emperor and then deposed by his mother, became emperor again after his sister-in-law Empress Wei was removed with the title Tang Ruizong (唐睿宗)

Prince Taiping (太平公主): Daughter of Li Zhi and Wu Zetian, a favorite of her mother's, a formidable political force in court for decades

Tang Xuanzong Li Longji (唐玄宗李隆基): Third son of Li Dan, stage multiple coup d'états to become the unquestioned political leader of the Tang Empire with the title Tang Xuanzong (唐玄宗)

> *"Military operations must always be kept short so the winner prepares himself as if he was in constant danger and his execution must be swift. His preparation is like a drawn bow and his execution is similar to that of releasing the arrow."*

The Art of War, Chapter 5

《故善战者，其势险，其节短。势如扩弩，节如发机。》
孙子兵法第五章

HISTORICAL CONTEXT

When Wu Zetian, at the grand old age of sixty-seven, became the founding emperor of the Zhou Dynasty, she made her son Li Dan, the former Tang emperor, adopt Wu as his surname after hers. However, that was not nearly enough for the poor son to earn the trust of his mother. Wu Zetian went on to kill all the officials who had maintained contact with Li Dan after his abdication.

The troubles of Li Dan were compounded by the jealousy of a woman scorned. One of Wu Zetian's court ladies was in love with Li Dan, who met her affection with contempt and indifference. The court lady found a way to get back at him when she accused two of Li Dan's consorts of performing sorcery, a crime for which they could be easily framed.

On the second day of the Lunar New Year, Li Dan's two consorts visited their mother-in-law to pay their respects and never returned to their palaces. Their loved ones might have vanished into thin air, but Li Dan and his children went about their business as if nothing had happened. This extraordinary feat of not noticing had probably saved their lives.

While her husband Li Zhi was on his deathbed, Wu Zetian moved to shore up the influence of her clan. Most significantly, she made her nephew, who harbored ambitions of becoming the crown prince, king of a vassal state and prime minister.[1] Wu Zetian as emperor was torn between choosing her heir from her own children and from her nephews. What was it going to be — a Li's dynasty or a Wu's dynasty? It was her loyal official[2] who helped her make up her mind.

---

[1] Wu Zetian's nephew was named Wu Chengsi (武承嗣) and was made the King of the vassal state Wei (魏). Wu Chengsi had his ambitions to be the crown prince and he had his faction grant more titles to his aunt Wu Zetian: that way, it solidified the concept that the Zhou Dynasty founded by his aunt was an empire ruled by Wu Zetian's maiden family, the Wu clan.

[2] The official's name was Di Renjie (狄仁杰). Di Renjie came from a prominent family, and his grandfather was a chancellor. He himself rose to the same level of esteem during

The official's argument was more metaphysical than practical: after Wu Zetian's death, only her own children would worship her in the temple and feed her and her late husband with sacrifices. Have you ever heard of nephews worshipping their aunts? The official asked and concluded that if someone from the Wu family became emperor, both Li Zhi and Wu Zetian would become hungry ghosts. The most powerful woman in Chinese history, as it turned out, was not immune from fear about what would happen to her after death. She made her third son Li Zhe, whom she had exiled, the crown prince.

Li Zhe, not the fourth son Li Dan, was chosen for good reasons. Li Zhe had been removed from the center of power for a long time[3] with no interaction with the top officials in the capital. That meant there had been no bad blood between him and members of the Wu clan. And, always a strategic thinker, the female emperor knew there was no better way to earn the loyalty of a prince who had fallen from grace than making him the future ruler of the country. That he was her eldest surviving son must have played a role too. In the zero-sum game of imperial succession, when one rises, the other must fall. Wu Zetian's nephew, upon hearing the news of Li Zhe's return, abandoned all hopes of becoming the crown prince and died shortly.

THE COUP D'ÉTAT OF SHENLONG (神龙政变)

The naming of the crown prince, however, did not mean that the struggle for power would subside. Towards the end of Wu Zetian's life, the main influence in court was her two young lovers; a pair of brothers who had been offered to the female emperor from the harem of her own daughter Princess Taiping.[4] Their unchecked power eventually posed a threat to the royal family. The son of Li Zhe together with his sister and her husband were forced to commit suicide by Wu Zetian for

---

Wu Zetian's administration and had survived Wu Zetian's secret police who terrorized most of the top officials.

[3] Li Zhe was exiled from the capital Chang'an (modern day Xian) to a southern region in modern day Jiangxi (江西) from 684 AD and returned to the capital in 698 AD.

[4] Their names were Zhang Changzong (张昌宗) and Zhang Yizhi (张易之). They were also referred to as the fifth son (五郎) and the sixth son (六郎). It was recorded that Yang Zaisi (杨再思) once wrote of Zhang Yizhi: "They say that the sixth son resembles the lotus flower, I think not. It is the lotus flower which resembles the sixth son." <人言六郎似莲花，非也；正谓莲花似六郎>. One could only imagine how handsome he was.

speaking ill of the brothers.[5] Along the way, Princess Taiping's lover perished as well. The Li royal family, now under siege like never before and witnessing the declining health of the female emperor, decided to stage a coup d'état. They aligned with key senior officials and the leader of the imperial guards.[6] Li Dan, Princess Taiping, and even the passive Li Zhe all went along with the plan. Perhaps not surprisingly given the old age of Wu Zetian and the lack of real influence possessed by her young lovers, the coup succeeded in removing the female emperor from power. Defeated, the once-mighty Wu Zetian confessed that though she was the founder of her own Zhou Dynasty, she would rather be honored and remembered as an empress of the Tang Dynasty. Her wishes were granted — she would be celebrated by the Li descendants as the empress of Li Zhi.

Li Zhe, now emperor for the second time, soon found out what sibling rivalry in a royal household could mean. His younger brother Li Dan was the first among equals of vassal kings.[7] To go back further in time, while Li Zhe was in exile, Li Dan, as emperor, had been busy building his network and consolidating his power base in the capital. Then there was his sister Princess Taiping. She was the favorite child of Wu Zetian who never saw her as a threat or contender for the throne. Princess Taiping had a strong network in the inner court and was on excellent terms with many officials in the cabinet.

---

[5] Li Zhe and his wife Empress Wei's son Li Chongrun (李重润) along with his sister and her husband, who was from the Wu family, were forced to commit suicide. This case shows that towards the end of Wu Zetian's reign, her violence was not merely against the royal Li family of the Tang Dynasty. Even members of the Wu family, if not amenable to her desires, would also perish.

[6] The chief of the officials was Zhang Jianzhi (张柬之) and the leader of the imperial guards was Li Duozuo (李多祚). Zhang Jianzhi was previously sidelined by Wu Zetian, but Di Renjie strongly recommended him which changed the Empress' mind and she began to appoint Zhang Jianzhi to higher offices. Li Duozuo was not of Han race but was instead from the tribe of Mohe (靺鞨). Originating from the northeastern part of China, the Mohe people would eventually be known as the Jurchens and later the Manchurians, the ruling race of the Qing Dynasty. The fact that the head of the imperial guards in the capital was of a minority race demonstrates that the Tang system was extremely inclusive racially.

[7] Li Dan, who was previously emperor himself, was named Xiang Wang (相王) with the character *Xiang* (相) meaning to assist and *Wang* meaning king (王). Unlike the other vassal kings of the Tang Dynasty, his title was not of a certain area like Qi (齐) or Jin (晋) but rather a blanket title to reflect the fact that he assisted in process of the Tang Empire's restoration.

THE RISE OF EMPRESS WEI

After years of living dangerously in the shadow of his powerful mother, Li Zhe was a spent force with little appetite for confrontation. It was his ambitious wife who was spoiling for a fight. Life in exile was difficult and Li Zhe had come to rely on his wife, Empress Wei, who went into exile with her husband, for emotional support. Li Zhe was in such a constant state of fear that he could only sleep in the arms of his wife. In moments of weakness when he wanted to take his own life to put an end to his suffering, his wife would talk him out of it and ask him to pull himself together. When Li Zhe returned to the capital to assume the throne again, therefore, he was hard pressed to say no to his wife who wanted to put her people in high places.

But there was no way he could do it without putting himself on the spot. The Tang Dynasty, though an absolute monarchy, had rules and regulations to keep imperial power in check. Royal edicts had to go through the cabinet in order to be effective. The emperor could bypass this process, but he could not do it in secret for he had to write the edict in black rather than the usual imperial red. The officials recommended by Empress Wei were thus publicly known to be appointed in an unofficial way.

Politics makes for strange bedfellows. A staunch supporter of Empress Wei was another of Wu Zetian's nephews,[8] who had built a strong faction during his aunt's reign. His loyalty to Empress Wei, though, was not strictly political — they were having an affair which the Emperor Li Zhe apparently knew of and condoned. This might sound strange, but members of the Wu and Li families were often forced to marry one another, despite the fact that they were always competing for power and influence. Li Zhe and Empress Wei had a daughter together and the princess, who had all the love from her parents, made a demand that had no historical precedent — to be named the Crown Princess.[9] Such was the spirit of the times.

---

[8]This nephew of Wu Zetian's was Wu Sansi (武三思) who was responsible for many deaths of the Li royal family. Unable to become the heir to Wu Zetian, he nonetheless maintained great power and influence in the Tang court due to the intermarriages with the Li family.

[9]With Empress Wei's only son Li Chongrun (李重润) having been forced to commit suicide during Wu Zetian's reign for speaking ill of his grandmother's young lovers the Zhang brothers, her own surviving child was Princess Anle (安乐公主) who was married to Wu Sansi's son Wu Chongxun (武崇训). Not being satisfied with being just a princess and

This forced the hand of Li Zhe's crown prince, who did what his uncles and granduncles had done — strike preemptively by staging a coup d'état.[10] Only this time, the coup was poorly organized and was put down swiftly. Empress Wei used this opportunity to point an accusing finger at Li Dan and Princess Taiping whose strong support in the cabinet enabled them to emerge from the episode largely unscathed. The sons of Li Dan, though, were sent into exile, thus somewhat diminishing his influence in the capital. This emboldened Empress Wei, who, in an attempt to emulate her mother-in-law, began to co-chair cabinet meetings and perform ceremonies with the Emperor.

Not long afterwards, the Emperor Li Zhe died suddenly under suspicious circumstances. In *The Old Book of Tang*, it was only recorded that he died unexpectedly. In *The New Book of Tang* written in the Song Dynasty, however, he was described as being poisoned by his wife and their daughter. This reminds one of how Wu Zetian was similarly portrayed in the history books. It was obvious that Song's Confucian scholars and historians were politically motivated to vilify these powerful women who rocked the boat of an imperial regime dominated by men.

Regardless of how Li Zhe died, it was necessary to find an heir to the throne and establish a political equilibrium that could at least temporarily balance the power of the various factions. Since Li Zhe had not named an heir or written a will, the title was very much up for grabs by the powers that be. On Empress Wei's side, the key player was a female official who had been influential since the Wu Zetian era.[11] Representing the Li royal family was Princess Taiping who was the second most important member of the faction next to her older brother Li Dan.

---

looking down upon the crown prince Li Chongjun (李重俊) whose mother was merely a consort, Princess Anle demanded to be named the Crown Princess.

[10]The crown prince Li Chongjun's rebellion was put down swiftly, but he did manage to kill Wu Sansi and his son Wu Chongxun, the husband of Princess Anle. Crown Prince Li Chongjun had in any case assisted in the path of clearing the empire for the return of absolute Li royal family control.

[11]The female official was Shangguan Waner (上官婉儿), the surviving granddaughter of the official Shangguan Yi (上官仪) who had tried to convince Li Zhi (李治) to depose Wu Zetian. She was exiled for her grandfather's crimes but would return and gain the trust of Wu Zetian. She was an influential figure in court during Li Zhe's period as well. Ironically from a modern standpoint, it was her who was actively dissuading Li Zhe from naming Princess Anle to be the Crown Princess.

After much deliberation and negotiation, both sides agreed to install Li Zhe's sixteen-year-old son as emperor.[12] Since he was only a teenager, administrative powers were to be split between Empress Wei who was then the Empress Dowager and Li Dan as the regent. The Wei faction,[13] however, challenged this arrangement on the basis of decorum governing the interaction of in-laws. A minister loyal to Empress Wei pointed out that brothers and sisters-in-law must minimize their contact with each other, so as not to convey any impression of impropriety. Therefore, Li Dan and Empress Wei, as in-laws, should not engage in active, constant communication. This would prevent Li Dan from performing his duties as regent effectively. As if to make the point that actions speak louder than words, Empress Wei sent 50,000 more soldiers to guard the capital and installed her loyalists as generals of the imperial forces. She then ordered the soldiers to surround Li Dan's residence.

THE COUP D'ÉTAT OF TANGLONG (唐隆政变)

This set the stage for the rise of one of the most naturally gifted politicians in Chinese imperial history, the third son of Li Dan whose name was Li Longji. His mother mysteriously disappeared on the second day of the new year when she went to pay respects to her mother-in-law Wu Zetian. As a boy, Li Longji distinguished himself with precocious maturity.[14] When his mother went missing, he responded with stately calm and remarkable self-composure. When he was sent into exile, he again took it in stride. Upon his return to the capital, he took pains to cultivate a network of contacts that included royal guards and Buddhist monks who were connected to the highest echelons of the Tang society.

He decided to take on the powerful Empress Wei. He had a plan which he kept from his father and brothers, so as not to implicate them if it went awry. Instead, he confided in his aunt Princess Taiping and won her support. Also on his side were high officials who were famous for knowing which way the political

---

[12] The young man's name was Li Chongmao (李重茂).

[13] The vocal official from the Wei faction was Zong Chuke (宗楚客) whose mother was a distant relative of the Wu clan. He was primarily responsible for putting down Li Chongjun's rebellion and was a staunch supporter of Empress Wei.

[14] Li Longji's nickname when he was young was "Aman" (阿瞒), the child name of the formidable Cao Cao of the "Three Kingdoms Period", featured in Chapter 3. It was enough to describe the perception of the adults who interacted with him.

winds blew. Equally critical was the loyalty of the imperial guards.[15] Fortunately for Li Longji, they had been treated badly by the Wei family. The leader of the imperial guards let Li Longji know that he could depend on them. With everything in place, the time was ripe for Li Longji to make his move. In the ensuing attack he launched on the royal palace known as the Coup D'état of Tanglong, his political opponents Empress Wei and her favorite daughter were murdered.[16]

LI DAN BECAME EMPEROR THE SECOND TIME

Under such circumstances, it was a sure thing that the sixteen-year-old emperor, handpicked by Empress Wei, would have to abdicate. The question was who his successor would be. The natural choice was Li Dan, the most senior member of the royal family. As for the choice of the crown prince, the person who deserved most credit for the removal of Empress Wei was Li Dan's third son Li Longji. Li Longji was not the Emperor's eldest son and his mother not the empress. But given his achievement, talent and political clout, what would happen if he was denied the title of crown prince? It had been eighty-four years since Li Dan's grandfather Li Shimin (from Chapter 4) murdered his brothers and everyone remembered it as a cautionary tale. They agreed that the best way forward for the Li royal family was to let the strong son be the heir to the throne. Li Dan's oldest son concurred and Li Dan proceeded to make his third son Li Longji his heir.

Now there was only one person the new crown prince had to worry about — his aunt Princess Taiping. That the Princess had never lost favor with her powerful, paranoid mother Wu Zetian was testament of her political acumen and sharp survival instincts. Her long proximity to the center of power also enabled her to build up her power base inside the government. In fact, it was precisely her hold on power at the highest level that made Li Longji enlist her as an ally in the first place. In court, her assertiveness served as a contrast to the passivity of the Emperor Li Dan who always deferred to her and the Crown Prince Li Longji on issues of importance.

With no higher authority to rein them in, Princess Taiping and the Crown Prince were bracing for a showdown. As it turned out, it was Princess Taiping who went on the offensive by casting doubt on the Crown Prince's status as the legitimate heir. She even tried to persuade her older brother Li Dan to remove Li

---

[15] Liu Youqiu (刘幽求) and Cui Riyong (崔日用) were the officials who were supportive of Li Longji, along with the head of the imperial guards Chen Xuanli (陈玄礼).

[16] Shangguan Waner perished along with Empress Wei and Princess Anle in this conflict.

Longji. That she failed, despite the fact that Li Longji was truly not the ideal candidate who met all the usual requirements, demonstrated the breadth and depth of support a Crown Prince had in court. Indeed, the top senior officials were united in rejecting the idea of replacing the Crown Prince Li Longji.[17] If history was any guide, they said, replacing the Crown Prince would shake the very foundation of the empire.

To defuse the situation, Li Dan gave orders to send his sister Princess Taiping away from the capital and grant additional administrative power to the Crown Prince Li Longji. Not one to admit defeat even in exile, Princess Taiping accused her nephew of intolerance and persecuting her. This put the Crown Prince on the defensive. He tried to demonstrate his filial piety by pleading in public for his aunt's return to the capital. To prove his sincerity, he even suggested to have his most loyal supporters executed as they were guilty of creating a gulf between him and his aunt. The emperor Li Dan deemed the punishment too severe and instead banished the ministers from the capital.

After returning to the capital, Princess Taiping began to play mind games with the Emperor Li Dan and tried to manipulate him into doing her bidding. She would cry in front of her older brother and urge him to appoint her people to the ministerial cabinet. She knew the Emperor had the authority to name ministers while the crown prince could only nominate middle and low-ranking officials. With "a little help" from the Emperor, her faction would gradually gain control of the main policymaking and executive bodies.

For a while, things seemed to be going her way until one day a meteor appeared in the west which, according to traditional beliefs, signified momentous change. Princess Taiping, sensing an opportunity, tried to move in for the kill. She told her older brother that the sign indicated that either the Emperor or the Crown Prince would be replaced shortly. This was a thinly disguised proposal to depose the Crown Prince. But to everyone's surprise and the Princess's great disappointment, Emperor Li Dan abruptly abdicated from his throne and named Li Longji as the new emperor. He himself would become the "supreme emperor".

---

[17] Yao Chong (姚崇) and Song Jing (宋璟) were the two officials who supported Li Longji. The two made a wonderful pair and were known to complement each other. It was said that Yao Chong was flexible with his methods and therefore was able to complete practical matters; while Song Jing was strict in his compliance with the rules and therefore was the anchor of the moral compass in court. (崇善应变以成务，璟善守文以持正)

THE COUP D'ÉTAT OF XIANTIAN (先天政变)

Li Longji might have become the new emperor, but the balance of power and political equilibrium in the court remained pretty much the same. As supreme emperor, Li Dan retained the authority to confirm the appointment of top officials. In fact, at the beginning of Li Longji's reign as emperor, most of the ministers in the cabinet as well as the heads of the imperial guards were from the Princess Taiping's faction. It was clear that unless some drastic action was taken, Li Longji would be an emperor in name only.

Worse still, two of his supporters who had urged Li Longji to take military action were exposed by their collaborator and sent into exile.[18] Li Longji got wind that the Supreme Emperor Li Dan had plans to send him to "inspect the borders", a euphemism for exile. This left Li Longji with little choice but to take matters into his own hands.

Things came to a head when an informant told Li Longji that Princess Taiping was plotting a coup d'état against him.[19] This may not have been true, but it was enough to help the young emperor make up his mind. A day before the alleged coup was supposed to take place, Li Longji sent three hundred men from his palace and disposed of the two pro-Princess Taiping generals of the imperial guards with the help of his younger brothers and brother-in-law. They then stormed into the cabinet's offices and killed the ministers that belonged to the Princess Taiping faction. The supreme emperor Li Dan fled with his main advisers. One of Li Dan's advisers was secretly partial to Li Longji and used the opportunity to convince Li Dan to hand over all his authority to his son. Princess Taiping's residence was surrounded and, three days later, the princess was forced to commit suicide.[20] Li Longji went on to lead the Tang Dynasty into one of its

---

[18]The two supporters who suggested a coup d'état were Liu Youqiu (刘幽求) and Zhang Yue (张说) and they were exposed by their collaborator Zhang Wei (张暐). Zhang Yue would thrive in Li Longji's era and when the emperor was to visit Mountain Tai (泰山), symbolizing that he had already attained greatness for the country, Zhang Yue used the opportunity to help his son-in-law to rise up the ranks. The phrase "the force of Mountain Tai" (泰山之力) was since used to refer to someone receiving help from his father-in-law. It makes one ponder how many people have been fortunate enough to possess such luck.

[19]One of Li Dan's men Wei Zhigu (魏知古), who was secretly partial to Li Longji, told the emperor Li Longji that Princess Taiping was plotting a coup d'état against the emperor on the fourth day of the seventh month of that year.

[20]Wei Zhigu (魏知古) and Guo Yuanzhen (郭元振) were both following Li Dan as he was fleeing that day. Since Wei Zhigu was already on Li Longji's camp, he used the

most glorious periods (713–755 AD) and presided over its rapid decline and fall precipitated by the An Lushan Rebellion (755–763 AD).

ANALYSIS

"Military operations must always be kept short so the winner prepares himself as if he was in constant danger and his execution must be swift. His preparation is like a drawn bow and his execution is similar to that of releasing the arrow."

The Art of War, Chapter 5

Li Longji differentiated himself from his father and aunt by exhibiting three key features that accounted for his success in the court rivalry: clear objective, preparation without demonstration of intent, and swift action. He thrust himself into the center of Tang court rivalries by plotting the removal from power of Empress Wei. The boldness of this operation was only matched by the meticulousness of its preparation. He never gave any hint about his thoughts on Empress Wei and was therefore able to stay under the radar as he proceeded with his plan. He took great pains to win the imperial guards over to his side as he knew their support would decide the outcome of the final showdown in the capital.

Perhaps most cunningly, he aligned himself with his aunt Princess Taiping rather than sharing his plans with his father Li Dan and his older brothers. Without involving them, Li Longji was poised to assume the title of crown prince after the revolt as he was the only male member of the Li family who could claim credit for the action.

Li Longji never lost sight of the big picture. He knew the supreme leader must also be the guardian of social values and moral virtues. His father, the Emperor Li Dan and Princess Taiping might have been his political opponents, but they were also his elders to whom he had to show respect. That was filial piety and why he had gone so far as to suggest the execution of his own people whom he held responsible for antagonizing his aunt.

When he decided that Princess Taiping posed a genuine threat to his authority, he plotted to annihilate her and did it in secret without arousing her suspicion. With swift action, like releasing the arrow from a drawn bow, Li Longji eliminated Princess Taiping and seized power from his father Li Dan. The flawless execution was comparable to the hunting process of the crocodile or leopard. The predator

---

opportunity to convince Li Dan to defer all authority to his son the emperor. Li Dan, realizing that he had lost control of the situation, agreed with Wei Zhigu on the suggestion.

would hide in the water or the bush and wait for its prey to come close. Then it would move in for the kill with a single and swift bite on the neck of its prey.

That reminds one of another Emperor with unerring predatory instincts. As written in Chapter 4 of *The Art of War*, "the skillful fighter puts himself into a position which makes defeat impossible and does not miss the moment for defeating the enemy." Wu Zetian was such a fighter. She would never strike unless she was certain that she would win. This made her path to the throne a long and winding process. She made her third son Li Zhe emperor. After deposing him, she was in no hurry to name herself as emperor. Instead, she chose her youngest son Li Dan to succeed his elder brother. It was only when the timing was completely in her favor did she ascend to the throne.

By so doing, however, she also sowed the seed of political turmoil in the future. The sky could not have two suns: when Wu Zetian handed over her power to Li Zhe, Li Dan found himself in an impossible position. What was the court to do with a man who was once the emperor? For the incumbent emperor Li Zhe, Li Dan would be an eternal threat and a cloud on the horizon.

Wu Zetian treated her political opponents, whether they were their children or from her own clan, with the same ruthlessness. For instance, both Empress Wei's son and the Wu family member who married a Li princess had to pay with their lives for speaking ill of her lovers. The Wu and Li families were therefore united in their struggle to survive Wu Zetian and, towards the end of her life, her inner circle.

That Wu Zetian, against all odds, became the only female emperor in Chinese history made things even more complicated. As a trailblazer, she demonstrated how far a woman with brains, ambition, and determination could go in politics. The emboldening effect this had on the women who came after her cannot be overstated. If early Tang court was overcrowded with contenders for power, it was partly because women like Empress Wei and Princess Taiping no longer considered politics a game only for men.

But none of these women was in the same league as Wu Zetian. Wu Zetian gained power by exerting influence over her sick husband Li Zhi who, despite his poor health, ruled his country uninterrupted during his reign. In sharp contrast, Empress Wei's husband Li Zhe had been sent into exile before he became emperor again and had to contend with the influence of his younger brother Li Dan who had also been emperor. Wu Zetian spent decades consolidating her power and running the country while her husband was lying sick. Empress Wei had neither the patience nor skills for this kind of power building. In trying to impose her will upon the government after the death of her husband, she made the fatal mistake of underestimating her political rivals: Li Dan and Princess Taiping.

If anyone could learn from Wu Zetian, it was her favorite child Princess Taiping. As a daughter, she had no legitimate claim to the throne and therefore posed no threat to her mother. Wu Zetian saw her more as a confidant and protégé. Princess Taiping used her special status to build her faction and influence in court. In time, she became such a strong presence in the capital that both her brothers, Li Zhe and Li Dan, had to treat her with respect even after their ascendance to the throne.

Given her clout and the influence she wielded in court, it was natural for the princess to want to have a say in the government when her nephew Li Longji was granted the title of crown prince. What she lacked, however, was a clear objective. She kept pushing forward without knowing where she wanted to go, so in the end she could not finish what she had started. She refused to back down as her nephew steadily gained in power, first as crown prince and later as emperor. Was it her ultimate objective to depose Li Longji and claim the throne herself, and become, like her mother, another female emperor of China? Did she really believe that lighting would strike twice for women in a country so overwhelmingly dominated by men? This reminds one of an important art form in Chinese culture: calligraphy. In order to write a character inside the box for regular script, a calligrapher must know the positioning of the last stroke before he begins writing the first. Princess Taiping proved to be a poor calligrapher in politics.

Li Dan was a master survivor during his mother's reign. Even with the disappearance of two of his consorts, he and his children were able to maintain a level of calmness as if nothing had happened. His passivity was what allowed him to survive in such tough circumstances. Because of his status and longevity, he was naturally pushed to be the emperor when Li Longji and Princess Taiping removed Empress Wei from power. He then used the same unassertive maneuvers when dealing with the rivalry between his son and sister. Not wanting to offend either party, he yielded to whomever had a request for him at the time. Similar to his sister Princess Taiping, Li Dan did not have an overall vision and execution strategy in terms of how he would like the balance of power to function. Since Princess Taiping was the more aggressive player in her fight with Li Longji, Li Dan repeatedly yielded to his sister. By balancing the two forces, he was using the same survival skills to maintain control and power. However, he failed to realize that his mother was not present anymore when he became the emperor again. There was no higher authority above him and his ambivalence would in fact bring additional disaster to the Li household. Since it would not be desirable for

Princess Taiping to have complete control of the regime, Li Dan's balancing act of using his sister as a counterweight against Li Longji meant that the margin of error was extremely small. Li Dan's inability to allow himself to rise to the position of authority, which was rightly and firmly his, meant disaster for both his sister and himself. His submission to Princess Taiping tipped the scales of the balance of power that forced the hand of Li Longji. Moreover, due to the violent nature of his removal of Princess Taiping, Li Longji eventually had to put Li Dan under semi-house arrest when he lost power; an outcome which was suboptimal for anybody's final years.

Hong Taiji

Nurhaci
【Founder of Qing Regime】

Daisan

Manggultai

HONG TAIJI
(Emperor Of Qing)

Nephew of

Amin

Chapter 7

Tender Care & Iron Fist: The Weapons of Hong Taiji

Dynasty: Qing Dynasty (清)

Period: circa 1620 AD to 1640 AD

Key Players:
Nurhaci: Effective founder of the Qing Regime

Daisan: Second son of Nurhaci, the most senior of the four great princes

Amin: Nephew of Nurhaci, second in seniority amongst the four great princes

Manggultai: Fifth son of Nurhaci, third in seniority amongst the four great princes

Hong Taiji: Eighth son of Nurhaci, most junior of the four great princes, later Emperor of Qing

"The leader uses mercy to gather support and then commands his supporters with discipline."

The Art of War, Chapter 9

《故令之以文，齐之以武。》

孙子兵法第九章

HISTORICAL CONTEXT

The Qing Dynasty wrested control of the vast land of China from the Ming Dynasty (1368–1644 AD) and ruled the country as its last imperial dynasty for 268 years from 1644 to 1912 AD. The regime was led by the Manchurians, a nomadic tribe from northeastern China.[1] Its founding father was Nurhaci who unified the Manchurian race and established a regional regime in 1616 AD that would eventually grow into the Qing Empire.[2]

His military success could be attributed to his superior organization skills: he grouped his men under banners of four different colors: yellow, white, red, and blue. Each soldier was placed under the command of one banner, in the same way that Manchurians followed a sign from their leaders when they were hunting for wild animals.[3]

---

[1] Their roots could be traced to the Jurchens (女真人) who founded the once-mighty Jin Dynasty (金) (1115–1234 AD). After Genghis Khan tore the regime to pieces, what remained of the Jurchen clan stayed in northeastern China as a semi-independent tribe which grudgingly pledged allegiance to the Ming Dynasty (明) (1367–1644 AD) because of its military superiority.

[2] One of the tribal military posts Jianzhou Zuowei (建州左卫) was led through the generations under the Ming by the Aisin-Gioro clan. The Aisin-Gioros were loyal subjects to the Ming but their father and son leaders Giocangga and Taksi were murdered in a military operation conducted by the Ming general of Korean Descent Li Chengliang (李成梁) in 1583 AD. Taksi's eldest son Nurhaci, then twenty-four, led whatever was left of Jianzhou Zuowei's men and resources on a path to avenge his father and grandfather and also to create a platform for himself and his Jurchen race. He was to be the founder of the Jin Khanate, later the Qing Empire.

[3] It is interesting to note that during the Qing Dynasty when the Manchurians had conquered all of China, it was a Manchurian official's privilege to call himself slave to the emperor. Han Chinese officials were only allowed to call themselves subjects to the Emperor. The title of slavery, rooted in the banner system, was seen as a status symbol. In any case, this tight banner organization during the Manchurian's path of expansion allowed

Nurhaci relied heavily on his sons and brothers[4] to fight alongside him in his quest for additional land and resources. As he got older, Nurhaci had to choose from his sons an heir to rule his nascent dominion. The Manchurians, unlike Han Chinese, did not have any clear, fully spelled-out rules of inheritance. Nurhaci's sons fought with their father with equal devotion but were treated very differently according to the relative status of their mothers' families. Unlike his counterpart in Han China, a Manchurian nobleman did not have a main wife but important consorts whose sons all had superior birthrights. Not only did their mothers come from influential Manchurian families, they had also been actively involved in their father's campaigns from a young age.[5] The other sons whose mothers were not of noble birth had been sidelined. Nurhaci's regime was a hybrid organization: his brother and sons were each given their share of human and animal resources, but all had to pledge their allegiance to Nurhaci. The resulting tension that existed between separation and unity would finally lead to bloodshed in the Aisin-Gioro clan for generations to come. As he grew older, Nurhaci had to select from his sons an heir to rule his growing empire.

The natural choice was the eldest son[6] whose mother came from a prominent family and who himself had actively participated in Nurhaci's early conquests. But his arrogance and difficult personality made him hugely unpopular with his brothers and senior officials. As the eldest son and the heir apparent, he would summon his younger brothers and tell them that when he succeeded their father, he would take away their property. Nurhaci found out about this and reprimanded him. But instead of mending his ways, the unrepentant eldest son had people perform voodoo on his father and younger brothers. When this came to Nurhaci's knowledge, he was furious and sentenced his eldest son to solitary confinement. The prince died in captivity two years later.

Nurhaci and his family to have a greater command of their soldiers and optimized their military effectiveness.

[4] His had relied heavily on his younger brother Surhaci to fight alongside him but eventually there came a time when Surhaci wanted to go his own way. Nurhaci, not one to tolerate defiance, arrested his younger brother who soon perished in captivity.

[5] Nurhaci's key sons who had assisted him in the establishment of his regime are as follows:

> First son Cuyen whose mother was Lady Tunggiya
> Second son Daisan whose mother was also Lady Tunggiya
> Fifth son Manggultai whose mother was Lady Fuca
> Eighth son Hong Taiji whose mother was Lady Yehenara

[6] Cuyen.

Shortly afterwards, Nurhaci increased the number of banners from four to eight and put his many sons and grandsons in charge. The four most powerful banner leaders were, in order of seniority: his second son Daisan, nephew Amin, fifth son Manggultai and eighth son Hong Taiji. They were collectively known as "the Four Great Princes".[7] Of the four princes, Daisan was the first among equals. As his son was in charge of another banner, Daisan was the de facto commander of two banners, like his father Nurhaci. They took monthly turns running the Manchurian dominion under the supervision of Nurhaci. Having established the balance of power, Nurhaci proceeded to establish his own regime.[8] As he became senile, he stipulated that after he passed away, the regime had to be governed by an oligarchy formed by the leaders of the eight banners.

DEATH OF NURHACI AND HIS SUCCESSION

Nurhaci died at the age of sixty-seven.[9] The vision he had for his empire to be jointly ruled by the leaders of the eight banners in harmony would prove to be

---

[7] On top of the original yellow, red, white, and blue banners, Nurhaci added the striped yellow, striped red, striped white, and striped blue. That was the origin of the term "eight banner man" (八旗子弟) synonymous with Manchurians up to the end of the Qing dynasty in 1912 AD.

The distribution of power by banner was as follows:

Nurhaci led both yellow and striped yellow banners;

Daisan, the oldest surviving son of Nurhaci, led the red banner;

Daisan's son Yoto led the striped red banner;

Hong Taiji led the white banner;

Dudu, son of Cuyen, led the striped white banner;

Manggultai led the blue banner; and

Amin, son of Surhaci (younger brother of Nurhaci), inherited his father's resources and led the striped blue banner.

The four most powerful banner leaders Daisan, Amin, Manggultai and Hong Taiji were known collectively as the Four Senior Beiles (四大贝勒: beile means prince in Manchurian).

[8] In 1616 AD, Nurhaci named his dominion, which covered modern-day northeastern China (东北) north of Beijing, the Jin Empire (金). Nurhaci named himself Khan (大汗), rather than emperor, in a nod to the nomadic Mongolian tradition. The Jin was to be the predecessor of the Qing dynasty (清).

[9] Nurhaci died a few months after the first major military defeat in his life in The Battle of Ningyuan (宁愿大战) against the Ming general Yuan Chonghuan (袁崇焕) who used cannons imported from Portugal to fight the mighty Manchurian cavalry.

unrealistic as soon as the founder of the regime breathed his last breath. He did not name a successor and infighting amongst the brothers and nephews ensued. After a series of intense discussion within the family, Hong Taiji, the youngest of the four great princes, was chosen as the new ruler.

WHY NOT DAISAN?

Daisan, the most senior of the four great princes, commanded an army comparable to that of his father's. To all appearances, he was the best choice to inherit the throne and was once named the successor. However, it only took a few false moves on his part to ruin his political future.

First it was the relationship he had with his father's main consort, who would go to banquets where Daisan was present wearing her best clothes and extra make-up. Then the two would exchange flirtatious glances. The relationship between the young wife of an elderly and powerful father and his young son was a sensitive subject and Daisan did not have the good sense to navigate himself out of troubled waters. The tipping point was reached when one of Nurhaci's young concubines told her master that the main consort had prepared meals for both Daisan and Hong Taiji: Daisan ate with much enjoyment while Hong Taiji refused to consume the meal. When Nurhaci heard about this, he never looked at his second son the same way again. Was Hong Taiji the person who told Nurhaci's young concubine? Otherwise, how would she know that Hong Taiji was the one who did not eat the meal from his stepmother? History would not give us an answer but Hong Taiji had a clear motive to plant this piece of intelligence into his father's mind.

Greed knows no bounds and that was exactly Daisan's problem. As his empire continued to expand, Nurhaci would, from time to time, give his sons and nephews new plots of land. Daisan was unhappy that the land he was given was no better than others. As the most senior of the great princes, he thought he deserved the best. To pacify Daisan, Nurhaci gave his own residence to him. Daisan might have gained a grand residence, but how could that be compared to the domains of the Manchurian regime?

However, it was how he treated his sons that became the final nail in the coffin. His three oldest sons[10] were all fierce warriors who had played a key role in the rise of the Manchurian regime and gained the favor of their grandfather Nurhaci. But they were treated with contempt and abuse by their stepmother and Daisan made the fatal mistake of siding with his new bride. When Nurhaci found

---

[10] Daisan's three warrior sons were Yoto, Soto, and Sahaliyan.

out about this, he was furious and reprimanded Daisan, who showed his remorse by killing the woman. That, however, was not enough for him to regain his father's favor, or his sons' support, which, as events unfolded, would have disastrous consequences for Daisan's political fortunes.

WHY NOT AMIN?

The second prince Amin was not Nurhaci's own son, but the son of his younger brother. He was therefore never seriously considered for the throne.

WHY NOT MANGGULTAI?

With Daisan and Amin out of the running, the most senior of princes was Nurhaci's fifth son Manggultai whose military exploits were just as impressive as those of his older brother Daisan's. However, he made one false move that proved to be his undoing. His mother had fallen out of favor with her husband Nurhaci and was demoted from the status of main consort. In a bizarre attempt to demonstrate loyalty to his father, Manggultai killed his own mother. Not only did this heinous act disgust Nurhaci, but the entire royal family was outraged. How could a person capable of murdering his own mother be the leader of the Manchurians? If he could do this to the one who gave birth to him, how would he treat his brothers and cousins?

WHY HONG TAIJI?

Hong Taiji was the eighth of Nurhaci's eighteen sons.[11] When his older brothers like Daisan and Manggultai were away for battles, he was left at home to take care of

---

[11] Hong Taiji's mother was named Monggojerjer from the Yehenara clan. The Yehenara tribe had been a formidable foe to Nurhaci's Aisin-Gioro clan and the marriage was meant to help the rivals make peace with each other. Nurhaci showered Monggojerjer, sixteen years his junior, with love and respect. Together they only had one son: Hong Taiji. Monggojerjer also took care of Daisan's oldest son Yoto. However, the personal relationship between Nurhaci and Monggojerjer could not alter the reality that the Aisin-Gioro and Yehenara clans were destined for a total war in their bid to be the ultimate master of the Manchurian race. When the war actually broke out between them, Monggojerjer fell seriously sick and wanted to see her Yehenara family one last time. Her Yehenara clan, however, decided to disown her since she had married their most formidable rival. Monggojerjer died in despair. Hong Taiji was only eleven at the time.

his younger brothers and nephews. Legends had it that he began to run the Manchurian royal household when he was only seven, managing its finances and nurturing the well-being of his younger relatives. Unlike his other Manchurian family members, he had a keen interest in history. For him, history held many lessons not only for the expansion of the Manchurian regime but his own rise to power.

When Nurhaci launched an offensive against the mighty Ming Empire, for example, it was Hong Taiji who proposed to have a few Manchurian spies disguised as horse merchants to gather intelligence in the enemy territory.[12] This greatly impressed his father and gave him the necessary military credentials to be named one of the great princes.

Most critical for his success was his popularity with the younger princes. Since Hong Taiji was the oldest of the princes who stayed behind and played the role of caretaker in the household while the older princes went to war, the younger princes had gotten used to seeing him as their leader. The sons of Daisan, in particular, regarded Hong Taiji, not their abusive father, as the worthy successor to their grandfather. It was their support that tipped the scales in the favor of Hong Taiji who was finally selected as the new ruler of the Manchurian regime.

POLITICAL EQUILIBRIUM IN HONG TAIJI'S EARLY REIGN

Having ascended to power, Hong Taiji moved swiftly to eliminate perceived threats and potential competition. One of the people on his radar was Nurhaci's last consort, guardian of the young sons of his late father, who had left them not only land but military resources.[13] A dominant mother could easily turn her teenage sons against their much older half-brother. Hong Taiji therefore decided to get rid of his stepmother. He fabricated evidence suggesting that Nurhaci wanted his last consort to be buried with him. No match for her ruthless and formidable stepson, Nurhaci's last consort died under dubious circumstances.[14]

---

[12] The first battle Nurhaci waged against the mighty Ming Empire was invading Fushun (抚顺) in modern day Liaoning (辽宁) in 1618 AD.

[13] Following the nomadic tradition, Nurhaci's property (the two yellow banners) was given to his youngest sons from his last main consort Abahai: Ajige aged twenty-one, Dorgon aged fourteen and Dodo aged twelve at the time of their father's death. The older ones did not share the last of the father's assets as they had already been allocated their share of the resources. The two banner leaders were Ajige and Dodo. Dorgon accordingly was subordinated to them.

[14] The thirty-seven-year-old Abahai either died from hanging herself or from being suffocated by the string of a bow; this was most likely witnessed by her adolescent sons.

But there were other, much larger obstacles to overcome in Hong Taiji's quest for absolute power. Under the arrangements put into place by Nurhaci, Hong Taiji had to share power with his many brothers and cousins. In fact, in the beginning of Hong Taiji's reign, the four great princes were seated side by side on thrones and received officials at court meetings together. They also took turns to take the driver's seat, so to speak. In other words, notwithstanding the title of ruler, Hong Taiji had no real authority over his older brothers and cousin.[15] On the contrary, he had to pledge allegiance to them and swear that he would never take away their properties.

GROOMING YOUNG PRINCES AND HAN OFFICIALS

Under Hong Taiji's leadership, the young Manchurian regime grew in both size and power. He led successful expeditions against Korea and Mongolia in the first years of his reign. Unlike his father, he usually prevailed over his enemy not by superior military strength or brute force but by brilliant tactics and strategies. The framing of a Ming general was a case in point.

Resisting the Manchurian advance on the more prosperous lands of the Ming regime was a Ming general who built strong fortresses with heavy artillery imported from Portugal. Rather than fighting the Ming general[16] head on, Hong Taiji went around the cities defended[17] by him and his Portuguese cannons and led the Manchurian forces to besiege the Ming regime's capital Beijing. This forced the Ming general to take his army back to Beijing and the two forces fought fiercely outside the city.

---

[15] The distribution of influence at the beginning of Hong Taiji's reign were as follows:

> Hong Taiji and his son eldest Hooge led two yellow banners (Hong Taiji's white banner was switched in color with Ajige, Dorgon and Dodo's banners as yellow reflected the khan's leadership. Cuyen's son Dudu who led the striped white banner was moved to be under the red banner and the original striped white banner, now striped yellow was granted to Hong Taiji's oldest son Hooge.).
> Ajige, Dorgon and Dodo led the two white banners.
> Daisan and his son Yoto led the two red banners.
> Manggultai led the blue banner.
> Amin led the striped blue banner.

[16] Yuan Chonghuan (袁崇煥).
[17] The northeastern cities of Ningyuan (宁远) and Jinzhou (锦州) in modern day Liaoning (辽宁).

While unable to defeat the general in battle, Hong Taiji found a way to eliminate his enemy without shedding a single drop of blood. He deliberately let Ming captives overhear a conversation concerning the general's collusion with the Manchurian forces. It was, of course, a set-up, but it worked. The Ming Emperor[18] ordered the execution of the general by a thousand cuts. By rewarding loyalty with such extreme cruelty, the Ming Emperor disincentivized every Ming military commander, leading to the fall of the empire.

This was not just pure luck. Hong Taiji proved himself to be well versed in the art of war. In Chapter Six of *The Art of War*, Sun Tzu writes, "Just as water flows downward, a military force must attack the weak and avoid the strong." By avoiding the artillery-protected fortresses and attacking Beijing, which was the heart of the Ming regime, Hong Taiji was able to circumvent the strong and strike at the underbelly of the enemy.

On the home front, Hong Taiji chose not to confront the great princes directly. Instead, he created separate power centers that competed with them. By doing so, he achieved his goal by killing two birds with one stone: new political forces created by him would naturally be loyal to him only and they provided fuel for the regime's expansion. One key political force that he relied upon was the younger princes like his son, his younger brothers, and his nephews.[19] By giving these young men opportunities to shine, Hong Taiji conveyed the impression of tolerance and impartiality. It also took the spotlight away from Daisan, Amin, and Manggultai which reduced their clout in policymaking.

Hong Taiji also won the loyalty of a group who had long been marginalized: the Han people who had been captured or had surrendered to the Manchu regime. Nurhaci practiced a tough policy on Han captives; they were made slaves to the Manchurian elites. Hong Taiji thought differently. Treating them well, he believed, would be of vital importance if the Manchurians were to be the ruler of the great Chinese land mass populated mainly by the Hans. Hong Taiji therefore allowed them to take the Confucian imperial examination similar to the one administered by the Ming regime. The top scorers were invited to join the Manchu government.[20] For the Han people who made up the majority of the population, respecting Confucianism meant respecting their culture. Holding

---

[18] Emperor Chongzhen (崇禎), the last emperor of the Ming Dynasty (明朝).

[19] The ones he relied most upon were his eldest son Hooge, his younger brother Dorgon (son of Nurhaci's last consort Abahai), and his nephew Yoto (son of Daisan).

[20] One of the most famous was Fan Wencheng (范文程) who was the descendant of the famous Northern Song chancellor Fan Zhongyan (范仲淹). Fan Wencheng went on to becoming a key adviser to Hong Taiji and helped him topple the Ming empire.

the Confucian classics and imperial examination in high regard goes a long way towards explaining why the Qing dynasty could last for 268 years while the other nomadic regime, the Yuan Dynasty, led by the Mongolians could only endure less than a hundred years. Moreover, the captured Ming soldiers were experts in operating Western cannons. Hong Taiji absorbed this talent and created the Han military banners with soldiers equipped with cannons and guns. Not only was this inclusion policy proved to be greatly beneficial for the Manchurian regime, but it was also another winner for Hong Taiji: these Han people were loyal to Hong Taiji solely.[21]

SUPPRESSING DAISAN

Having strengthened his power base and shored up his position, Hong Taiji moved confidently to remove his rivals. For that purpose, no cause would be too trivial. Daisan, as the eldest sibling, tried to play peacemaker in a quarrel between Hong Taiji and their sister. When Hong Taiji found out that his second eldest brother was going to meet with his sister,[22] he accused Daisan of conspiracy. At a meeting called to discuss the issue with the princes, he threatened to abdicate unless Daisan was duly punished. This put Daisan under tremendous pressure and eventually he had to beg Hong Taiji for forgiveness. Showing leniency, Hong Taijing only made Daisan promise that he would remain loyal in his position and not to have any disobedient thoughts.

SUPPRESSING MANGGULTAI

Then came Manggultai whose explosive temper played right into the hands of Hong Taiji. When asked to explain why a military operation he led did not go as well as planned, he lost his cool and got into a nasty row with Hong Taiji.

---

[21] The Han banner men also constituted a breeding ground of talent. The author of the great *Dream of the Red Chamber*, Cao Xueqin (曹雪芹), for example, was one of its members.

[22] When Hong Taiji conquered the Mongolian leader Ligdan Qayan, he gifted the defeated ruler's wives and daughters to his Manchurian princes as a reward. Hooge, Hong Taiji's eldest son, was one of the recipients. Hooge was already married to Hong Taiji's sister Mangguji's daughter. The princess Mangguji was naturally upset and she demonstrated her anger in the banquet that celebrated the defeat of the Ligdan Qayan by directly confronting her brother Hong Taiji, asking him how he could treat her daughter that way. The situation was awkward and Daisan, being the eldest brother in the family, tried to appease Mangguji by inviting her to his residence for dinner.

The hot-headed Manggultai took out his sabre and swung it in front of the Manchurian ruler. Hong Taiji was furious and reminded Manggultai of what a heinous crime he had committed in murdering his own mother. Having shamed him into submission, Hong Taiji stripped Manggultai of his title of great prince and had his own son take over his uncle's property and military force.

SUPPRESSING AMIN

Amin was the least threatening of the great princes. All he wanted was independence from the Manchurian regime ruled by the descendants of his uncle Nurhaci. That was why he harbored ambitions to be King of Korea when he invaded the country. He only dropped the idea because of the opposition from his co-commander.[23]

In the Battle of Beijing, the Manchurian army conquered four cities near the Ming capital and Amin was entrusted with the task of defending them. When the Ming army launched a counter-offensive with soldiers that far outnumbered Amin's forces, Hong Taiji sent reinforcements to his rescue. Before the relief troops arrived, however, Amin had already fled for his life. Hong Taiji was furious and punished Amin by confiscating his property and military resources. He also put Amin under house arrest until the fallen prince's death.

HONG TAIJI AS THE ABSOLUTE MONARCH

On paper, Hong Taiji was still one of the four great princes. But in terms of prestige, power and political clout, he was first among equals in court.[24] Three years after he had assumed the title of the Manchurian ruler, the four great princes no longer held office on a monthly rotating basis. The collective leadership of oligarchy was replaced by the one-man rule of Hong Taiji. Another three years passed and Hong Taiji became the only person seated on the throne looking down on his officials including the other great princes. He had succeeded in becoming the unquestioned and unrivalled authority of the Manchurian regime, though his untimely death would plunge the nascent Qing Empire into disarray just as his father Nurhaci had when he died.[25]

---

[23] Amin's co-commander was Dudu, son of Cuyen.

[24] Amin's striped blue banner was confiscated and was reallocated to his brother Jirgalang.

[25] Hong Taiji did not live to see his Qing empire take over the vast lands of China proper in 1644 AD. His untimely death in 1643 AD left the young Qing regime in turmoil. Hong

ANALYSIS

"The leader uses soft skills to gather support and then commands his supporters with discipline."

The Art of War, Chapter 9

This is an apt description of Hong Taiji's secret to success — tempering force with mercy, as well as knowing when to advance and when to retreat. As his older brothers were busy trying to prove themselves on the battlefield, Hong Taiji stayed behind to play the role of the caregiver, provider, and patriarch to the younger members of the royal extended family, attending to their various needs and solving their problems. This investment in personal relationships and *guanxi*

Taiji's death was sudden and, since the Manchurian succession system at that time was not sufficiently Confucian, none of his sons was the heir apparent. Worse still, the various banners could not agree on who should succeed the great Hong Taiji.

The red banners were controlled by the elderly Daisan and his sons. The striped blue banner was led by his cousin Jirgalang who, as Surhaci's son, was not eligible to be emperor. The yellow banners, loyal to Hong Taiji, wanted the successor to be a son of the late emperor. The formidable white banners led by Nurhaci's youngest sons Dorgon and Dodo disagreed. The one they supported was Dorgon, who had scored many military victories during Hong Taiji's reign. The discussion on this topic was so heated that the Aisin-Gioro brothers and cousins nearly got into a physical fight in the palace. Dorgon, always the clever one, proposed a solution: to satisfy the yellow banners, he nominated Hong Taiji's ninth son Fulin (福临) to be the emperor. Fulin's mother Bumbutai was from the great Mongolian family of Borjigit, the descendants of Genghis Khan. Since Fulin was so young, Dorgon himself and Jirgalang of the striped blue banner were to be prince regents assisting the emperor.

By giving up the throne in exchange for real power, Dorgon was able to get on top of a difficult and potentially explosive situation. Once he became prince regent, he led the Manchurian forces into China proper in 1644. Then he had his main rival, Hong Taiji's eldest son Hooge arrested on trumped-up charges and had him executed. Yet before he could wreak more havoc, Dorgon died in a horse-riding accident in 1650 AD at the age of thirty-eight.

This gave Fulin (the Emperor Shunzhi (顺治皇帝)) the long-awaited opportunity to emerge from his uncle's shadow. He took over the administrative power of the empire at fourteen. Determined to avenge his older brother Hooge, the Emperor Shunzi accused Dorgon posthumously of treason and had his remains flogged. Then he consolidated his power by seizing control of Dorgon's white banner and took over the two yellow banners as well. This is a lesson from history — never underestimate a well-trained fourteen-year-old's intent on gaining power.

paid off handsomely when, at a meeting held to select the Manchurian ruler after Nurhaci, Daisan's sons cast the swing vote in Hong Taiji's favor.

When Nurhaci was alive and he was just one of the four great princes, Hong Taiji never wavered in his loyalty to his father. He made no false moves while most of the wounds of his older brothers were self-inflicted. Like Iago in Shakespeare's *Othello*, Hong Taiji was a master of exploiting people's suspicious nature. There was good reason to believe that he was behind the ploy of letting his father Nurhaci know of Daisan's consumption of his stepmother's meal and this certainly eroded the father's affection for his second son. Hong Taiji used the same covert approach to deal with external threats. The mind game that he played on the Ming's emperor was a stroke of genius: he had his archenemy the Ming general killed at the hands of his own master. Destroying one's enemies without fighting would surely win the approval of Sun Tzu.

Hong Taiji was by no means the absolute ruler when he succeeded his father Nurhaci. But he continued to build his power base by mentoring the younger princes and promoting Han officials. This strengthened his regime and enhanced his own status and credibility. Tactically speaking, it was a no-lose situation for Hong Taiji, as ruler, could claim credit for himself or assign blame to others, depending on political expediency.

Hong Taiji was a natural born killer with unerring predatory instincts. He never hesitated to strike the fatal blow when he was in a position of strength and his enemy in a position of weakness. His actions remind one of a skilled hunter in the animal kingdom like a crocodile which would wait under water until its prey came sufficiently close. Then it would get surprisingly agile and explosively fast when it delivers a single fatal bite in the neck and drag the prey into its aquatic habitat. This combination of overt meekness, accumulation of power, and swift action allowed Hong Taiji to come out on top.

Fourth Prince Yinzhen

Kangxi
(Emperor of Qing)

Yinreng
(Second Prince/Crown Prince)

Yinsi
(Eighth Prince)

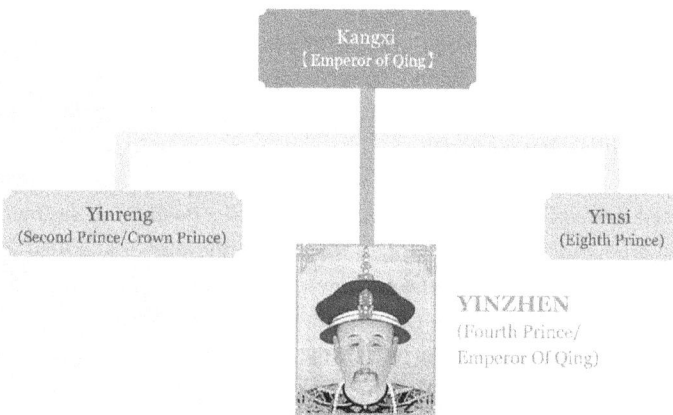

YINZHEN
(Fourth Prince/
Emperor Of Qing)

Chapter 8

Position of Invincibility: Yongzheng's Strategy to Success

Dynasty: Qing Dynasty (清)

Period: circa 1700 AD to 1730 AD

Key Players:

The Emperor Kangxi (康熙): Emperor of Qing with the title Kangxi (康熙皇帝)

Yinreng (胤礽): Second son of Kangxi, The Crown Prince

The Emperor Yongzheng Yinzhen (雍正皇帝-胤禛): Fourth son of Kangxi, low-profile and obedient, later Emperor with the title Yongzheng (雍正皇帝)

Yinsi (胤禩): Eighth son of Kangxi, popular amongst his brothers and officials, later purged by Yongzheng

"The winner places himself in an invincible position while never loses the opportunity to take advantage of the vulnerabilities of the enemy."

The Art of War, Chapter 4
《故善战者，立于不败之地，而不失敌之败也。》
孙子兵法第四章

HISTORICAL CONTEXT

Emperor Kangxi became the ruler of the Manchurian-led Qing Empire at the age of eight[1] in 1661 AD and was the longest-reigning monarch in Chinese history. By fighting off the Russians in the north, putting down the rebellion of the once-loyal Han generals in the south, taking back Taiwan in the east and expanding to Outer Mongolia in the west, Kangxi established himself as one of the most successful conquerors in Chinese and world history. His biggest challenge, though, was the management of the incessant rivalry among his sons as well as the conflict between his sons and himself.

SECOND PRINCE AS THE CROWN PRINCE

Not only was Kangxi the longest-reigning emperor in Chinese history, he also had the most male children — a total of thirty. His empress came from a politically

---

[1] The Emperor Shunzi (顺治), the first Qing ruler to reign over China proper, died at the age of twenty-four in 1661 AD from measles, an illness that plagued Manchurians who entered the Han area. He was succeeded by his third son Xuanye (玄烨) and his imperial name was Kangxi (康熙). Kangxi was then only eight years old but had already proven himself to be a survivor. He had been exposed to the disease and therefore developed an immunity. This prompted his grandmother the Empress Dowager Xiaozhuang (孝庄皇太后) to heed the advice of the Catholic priest Johann Adam Schall von Bell and name him as the emperor. The child Emperor was assisted by four minister regents appointed by the Emperor Shunzi. The four regents were Soni, Oboi, Ebilun, and Suksaha. Soni was a yellow-banner loyalist whose family Heseri was of great prominence. Kangxi would go on to marry Soni's granddaughter Lady Heseri (赫舍里氏). When Soni passed away, Oboi became the most senior of the regents. His power and influence continued to grow until he became a threat to the young emperor. At fourteen, Kangxi already had great plans for Qing and was not going to let anybody stand in his way. He had Oboi arrested and took complete control of the empire.

influential family and the two of them had a great relationship.[2] To Kangxi's chagrin, however, his empress died when she gave birth to their child who was his second son. Out of his love for the Empress, Kangxi named her son as the crown prince. Moreover, although of similar nomadic origins, the Manchurians showed much greater respect to the tradition of Han Chinese than the Mongolians who ruled China during the Yuan Dynasty (1271–1368 AD). A prominent example would be Kangxi's approach to succession planning.

Kangxi was partial to the Crown Prince and gave him the best Confucian education coupled with Manchurian horseback riding and archery training. Living up to his father's expectations, the Crown Prince excelled in both the classics and traditional Manchurian combat. As he got older, a faction was formed to defend and further his interests as the Crown Prince. Given his status, this development was inevitable, but it also alienated many of his brothers. With thirty sons, Kangxi faced a challenge to manage the sibling rivalry within his royal family. But he gave himself an almost impossible task when he condoned and even nurtured a highly competitive environment for his sons to interact with one another.

THE FALL OF THE CROWN PRINCE

The first sign of a split between Kangxi and his favorite son appeared when the Crown Prince was sixteen. Kangxi was fighting the Mongolians and the Emperor fell ill. Longing for his son's company, he summoned the Crown Prince to his army camp. To the Emperor's dismay, the Crown Prince did not show any sadness when he saw his sick, fragile father. This episode left a bitter aftertaste for Kangxi.[3] A few years later, the Emperor was off to another campaign and the Crown Prince was to stay in the capital to administer state affairs. Not before long, rumors began to circulate that the Crown Prince was not behaving obediently, and his actions strayed away from the parameters set by the Emperor. This put Kangxi on guard. In a move to offset the Crown Prince's increasing power and growing influence, he gave a number of his other sons princely titles.[4] As a result, people at the Qing court tended to fall into two camps: The Crown Prince and his faction versus other princes and their supporters.

---

[2] Kangxi's Empress was the noble Soni's granddaughter Lady Heseri.

[3] Kangxi was fighting the Galdan Mongols in 1690 AD in modern day Outer Mongolia.

[4] Kangxi named his fourth son Yinzhen (胤禛), fifth son Yinqi (胤祺), seventh son Yinyou (胤祐) and eighth son Yinsi (胤禩) as beiles, or junior grade princes in the Qing Empire.

A few years later, Kangxi removed a key minister[5] who was also the grand-uncle and a staunch supporter of the Crown Prince. The Emperor accused him of treason and had him arrested. The once-powerful official was thrown behind bars and executed by royal edict shortly after. Along with him, many officials who supported the Crown Prince were either imprisoned or put to death.

Kangxi and the Crown Prince's relationship became so strained that a minor incident could escalate into a full-blown crisis. Five years after the execution of the key minister, Kangxi went on a hunting trip with his sons. One of Kangxi's younger sons was seriously ill, causing much pain to the emotionally sensitive Emperor. The young prince soon died but the Crown Prince, again, showed only indifference. Kangxi berated the Crown Prince but the heir to the throne was unrepentant. The royal family continued its hunting trip and the Crown Prince, after being reprimanded, was seen peering into his father's camp at night. Convinced that the Crown Prince was planning something evil, Kangxi called for a meeting with the highest officials to depose his heir.

THE CROWN PRINCE RISES AGAIN

With the Crown Prince's fall from grace, all of Kangxi's other sons had a chance to become the heir. The frontrunner was the charismatic eighth prince who had the backing of a good number of his brothers, collectively known as the eighth prince faction. The Emperor also held him in high regard and at one time appointed him as the guardian of the imperial treasury.

However, the eighth prince's popularity proved to be his greatest liability. In an attempt to tip the scale in their favor, a brother[6] from the eighth prince faction

---

[5]The official's name was Songgotu, who was the son of Soni and uncle of Kang Xi's Empress Lady Heseri.

[6]The first prince Yinti (胤禔), for example, had the advantage of family backgrounds — his mother came from the prominent Yehenala family and his maternal uncle was the high-ranking official Mingzhu (明珠), who had greatly assisted Kangxi in his early years. But unfortunately Mingzhu had since fallen out of favor with the Emperor, depriving the first prince of much-needed political backing. The first prince also had a competitive streak that Kangxi, who prized family harmony above everything else, found off-putting. In fact, Kangxi disliked this son so much that he once declared that all princes could have a chance to be the heir except the first prince for he was stubborn and idiotic. Practically out of the running, the first prince threw his weight behind the eighth prince Yinzi, who had been raised not by his own mother of humble birth but by the first prince's noble mother. As such the first prince was partial to the eighth prince.

told the Emperor that, according to a fortune teller, the eighth prince was destined to be the next ruler. Moreover, he would be willing to kill the deposed crown prince if that was what it took to make that happen. This turned out to be a death blow to the eighth prince's bid for the title.

Kangxi might have been greatly disappointed in the deposed crown prince, but he did not want him dead, let alone murdered by his own brother. Bringing in the divine will was a kiss of death for the supposed chosen one. Emperors invariably saw it as a challenge to their earthly authority. This aroused Kangxi's suspicion further and led him to believe that a plot was brewing against the deposed crown prince.[7] At the meeting he called to discuss the issue, he had a confrontation with the princes who insisted on the innocence of the eighth prince. At one point, the Emperor was so irate that he drew his sword. Bloodshed was only avoided when a prince got down on his knees, grabbed his father's leg and begged for his forgiveness.[8]

After a month or so, an election, which only allowed officials[9] above a certain rank to vote, was held to select the new crown prince. Not surprisingly, the popular eighth prince received the most votes, not least from members of the Manchurian aristocracy. This worried Kangxi. If he had deposed the former crown prince because of the threat his power and influence posed to the imperial

---

[7] The third prince Yinzhi (胤祉) who was the most academic of the princes, struck a blow at the first prince by informing his father that the first prince had performed voodoo with a Mongolian monk on the crown prince. The third prince further elaborated that the fortune teller Zhang Mingde (张明德) who spoke in favor of the eighth prince, had hired assassins against the Crown Prince and had liaised with the eighth prince. The eighth prince threw him out of his residence out of fear but the plot against the Crown Prince was now even more linked with the eighth prince. After knowing this, Kangxi had the fortune teller executed with the method of death by a thousand cuts and put the first prince under house arrest for his ill-intentioned plans on the former crown prince.

[8] Knowing that the eighth prince was somehow implicated in a plot against the Crown Prince, his loyal younger brothers the ninth prince Yintang (胤禟) together with the fourteenth prince Yinti (胤禵) brought poison to convince their father of the eighth prince's innocence: if Kangxi did not believe them, they would take their lives on the spot. During the discussion, the fourteenth prince went into a brawl with his father and Kangxi was so irate that he drew his sword. Fortunately, the fifth prince was there to stop his father by grabbing his leg while kneeling down, preventing royal bloodshed in that instance. The fourteenth prince was then punished by being flogged twenty times.

[9] The eighth prince was supported by officials from prominent Manchurian families such as Tong Guowei (佟国维) of the Tunggiya clan, nephew of Kangxi's mother, brother of Kangxi's Empress, and Maqi (马齐) of the Fuca clan.

order, how could he let the eighth prince, apparently with even more power and influence, be the new crown prince?

Ignoring the election results, Kangxi claimed that he saw his grandmother the Empress Dowager and his late empress in his dream and that they looked distraught. He believed it was their way of telling him that he had made a mistake in removing the Crown Prince. His favorite son, therefore, was reinstated as crown prince while the eighth prince and his supporters were further sidelined.[10]

Notably absent from this intense power struggle was the fourth prince who kept a low profile during the election and wisely voted for the reinstatement of the Crown Prince.[11] By so doing, he demonstrated his loyalty not only to the Crown Prince but, more importantly, to his father.

THE SECOND FALL OF THE CROWN PRINCE

That Kangxi decided to have the Crown Prince reinstated did not mean he no longer regarded him as a threat. Nor could it be taken for granted that the newly reinstated crown prince would remain grateful and content. Quite the opposite. He was heard wondering aloud: Where in history could you find a person who remained a crown prince for forty years? A small incident would soon trigger an earthquake-level disturbance to the Qing Empire.

A member of the royal family died and in honor of him, Kangxi banned the consumption of alcohol for a few days.[12] Kangxi was then informed that twenty top officials participated in a banquet where liquor was consumed. These officials, including the head of the imperial guards, the minister of justice, and the minister of the military, all belonged to the crown prince faction.[13] Given the strategic positions they held, it was not inconceivable that they were planning a coup d'état.

---

[10] He accused Tong Guowei and Maqi of maliciously stirring up trouble and had them stripped of their ranks as chancellors. The eighth prince was sidelined and Kangxi even put Maqi, supporter of the eighth prince, as a prisoner under the eighth prince's surveillance. This forced the eighth prince to maintain a tight grip on his supporter Maqi. Kangxi's motive was to have the members in the eighth prince faction cannibalize each other.

[11] Along with the fourth prince, the thirteenth prince Yinxiang (胤祥) also voted for the reinstatement of the former crown prince. The fourth and thirteenth princes were to be lifelong partners in court politics.

[12] Ma Erhun (马尔浑), a member of the Aisin-Gioro royal family died in 1709 AD.

[13] The key officials in the banquet were the head of the imperial guards Tuo Heqi (托合齐), the minister of justice Qi Shiwu (齐世武) and the minister of the military Die (狄额).

While the tip-off, given by a member of the eighth prince's faction,[14] was clearly a move targeted at the crown prince's faction, Kangxi was convinced that the banquet was a cover-up for a plot to remove him from the throne and make the Crown Prince emperor. He ordered the arrest and execution of all the officials involved[15] and stripped the Crown Prince of his title. He also declared that he would have whoever suggested reinstating the fallen Crown Prince executed together with his extended family, and that he would not name any crown prince for the remainder of his years.

THE EIGHTH PRINCE & THE FOURTH PRINCE

While the eighth prince was happy to see his archrival removed, he failed to earn the trust of his father back. He once sent his father a gift, but what Kangxi actually received was a dead eagle. The Emperor saw it as a curse and never forgave his son. He withheld grain supply to the eighth prince and showed no compassion when the eighth prince fell seriously sick one year after the eagle incident.

A low-profile, almost reluctant contender for the position of crown prince was the fourth prince. The eldest of the princes still in active running for the title, the fourth prince apparently did not belong to any faction. He had demonstrated his loyalty to his father by pleading for the reinstatement of the Crown Prince. His self-effacement was informed by a piece of advice given by his closest adviser:

"If you don't show your talents, you'll be ignored.
If you show your talents too much, you'll be viewed with suspicion."

The fourth prince had kept a careful distance from the Crown Prince since his reinstatement. Unlike the eighth prince, he did not have a strong power base. But he had always stayed close to his father and away from political infighting. Buddhism, not politics, seemed to hold more interest for the fourth prince who maintained a cordial relationship with all his brothers.

---

[14] The informant was the younger brother of the deceased Ma Erhun, named Jingxi (景熙), who coincidentally was the brother-in-law of the eighth prince.

[15] Tuo Heqi was sentenced to death by a thousand cuts; fortunately for him, he died prior to the execution date. Qi Shiwu was nailed to the wall and could be heard wailing for a few days before dying.

Most importantly, the fourth prince demonstrated unwavering loyalty to his father. He knew what made his father happy. For example, he included Tibet[16] in the map of the Qing Empire when the territory was still up for grabs. This was a clever way of saying to the Emperor that his success was certain.[17]

In another instance, the eighth prince fell sick while on a hunting trip with the royal family. Kangxi told the fourth prince to go and visit him, then accused him of showing too much emotion during the visit and wondered whether the fourth prince was in fact a member of the eighth prince faction. Then he decided that the eighth prince should be brought back to the city. Despite the opposition of other princes to the move, the fourth prince, as usual, was obedient to his father to a fault. He saw to it that the eighth prince was escorted back to the city.

THE FOURTH PRINCE BECAME EMPEROR YONGZHENG

Kangxi died at the age of sixty-nine in his suburban palace. The circumstances of his death and the succession process to his throne remain mysterious to this day. Kangxi had sent the fourth prince to "sacrifice to the heavens", a ritual that was usually only performed by emperors, implying that the father might have had the intention to make his fourth son his successor early on.

---

[16] Including Tibet was a low-cost way for the fourth prince to earn his father's favor as he was not chosen to fight in the campaign. The eighth prince, knowing that he would not be able to be heir, instead supported a member of his faction, the fourteenth prince Yinti, to be the contender for the throne. The fourteenth prince was born of the same mother as the fourth prince though the brothers from the same mother were not close: the fourth prince was brought up by the empress Tunggiya while the fourteenth prince was raised by his birth mother. In 1718 AD, the fourteenth prince was named as the King general (大将军王) to lead the campaign in Tibet against the remaining forces of the Galdan Mongols. The fourth prince had wanted to contend for the position but had lost out to the fourteenth prince. The fourteenth prince was given the highest honors when he left for Tibet: the leading flag being the yellow banner and the rituals were according to the standards of the highest level of a Manchu aristocrat.

[17] Another thing in the fourth prince's favor was having one of his people in a key position. The main supplier of resources to the fourteenth prince in his campaign in Tibet was the viceroy of Sichuan (四川) named Nian Gengyao (年羹尧). Geographically, Sichuan was the agricultural province closest to Tibet and was therefore the lifeline to the fourteenth prince's troops. Nian Gengyao was a banner man of Han descent and he had served under the fourth prince within the banner structure. Nian Gengyao was therefore naturally loyal to the fourth prince which meant that the fourteenth prince was in effect within the purview of the fourth prince.

On the day he died, Kangxi ordered the fourth prince to return from the capital to his palace in the suburb. Then he called for the presence of other princes and the head of the imperial guards,[18] and allegedly told them that he had decided to name the fourth prince as the next emperor. The fourth prince arrived in the late morning to see his father, who died that evening. Then the head of the imperial guards announced that the fourth prince would be the next emperor with the imperial name Yongzheng.

Conspiracy theories abound on whether Kangxi had really chosen the fourth prince as his successor. This is not surprising, given the secrecy of both the selection and announcement process as well as the fact that the head of the imperial guards was the only independent witness. For example, rumor had it that the fourth prince had colluded with the head guard and made himself emperor. Regardless of what had actually happened, the opaqueness of Kangxi's successor selection and announcement process led to speculations which damaged the legitimacy of the imperial power.

It was exactly because his legitimacy was in doubt that the new emperor, now called Yongzheng, could not tolerate any challenge to his authority. Moreover, his political support was thin compared to that of the formidable eighth prince faction.

THE FATE OF THE OTHER PRINCES UNDER EMPEROR YONGZHENG

For the new Emperor Yongzheng, governing the country was a delicate balancing act. Initially, he tried to co-opt the eighth prince by reserving a top position for him in his cabinet. But the eighth prince faction proved to be unappeasable and it was not long before Yongzheng had to resort to more ruthless measures. On some trumped-up charges, he put the key members of the eighth prince faction under house arrest or sent them into exile. The unlucky ones would die during the

---

[18] With the fourteenth prince still at the front lines, Kangxi summoned the other main princes stationed in Beijing, namely the third prince Yinzhi (胤祉), the seventh prince Yinyou (胤祐), the eighth prince Yinsi (胤禩), the ninth prince Yintang (胤禟), the tenth prince Yine (胤䄉), the twelfth prince Yintao (胤裪), and the thirteenth prince Yinxiang (胤祥) to his residence. The only non-royal family member present was the head of the imperial guards Longkeduo (隆科多) who was the son of Tong Guowei of the Tunggiya clan.

thirteen years of Yongzheng's reign,[19] while the relatively fortunate princes would outlive Yongzheng and receive pardons from their nephew Emperor Qianlong (乾隆), son of Yongzheng, who did so for the purpose of earning a reputation for magnanimity early in his reign.[20]

THE SECRET SUCCESSOR SELECTION PROCESS AND PUBLIC ANNOUNCEMENT

Having observed at close range how violent imperial sibling rivalry could be, Yongzheng came up with a radically different approach to imperial succession that had no precedent in Chinese history. This approach, Yongzheng believed, would also bestow more legitimacy upon the chosen successor.

He created the "secret successor naming system" which was carried out as follows: the Emperor would write the name of his chosen successor on a royal edict and place it behind the plaque hung from the ceiling in the "Palace of Heavenly Purity" (乾清宮) in the Forbidden City.

Following the death of the emperor, a eunuch would read the name of the selected heir out aloud. The four subsequent emperors were all chosen in such a fashion. The last three Qing emperors, however, were children when they ascended to the throne and they remained childless at their death. The secret successor naming system, therefore, had no use to them. Since Qing was the last imperial regime in China, we would not know whether this selection system could stand the test of time beyond a few generations.

ANALYSIS

> "The winner places himself in an invincible position while never loses the opportunity to take advantage of the vulnerabilities of the enemy."

> *The Art of War, Chapter 4*

---

[19] Both the eighth and the ninth princes were forced to change their names to "Akina" and "Seshe" which could mean animal and irritating respectively. The two princes were to perish in house arrest under dire circumstances.

[20] The tenth prince was also exiled but managed to outlive Yongzheng and was released when Yongzheng's son Qianlong assumed the throne. The fourteenth prince rushed back from the front line in the northwest as soon as he heard of his father's passing and was in such shock that Kangxi had chosen his fourth brother to be emperor that he refused to bow to the new ruler Yongzheng. His lack of respect to the emperor resulted in his house arrest for the entirety of the thirteen years of Yongzheng's reign and was subsequently released when his nephew Qianlong became emperor.

Loyalty was the fourth prince's defining character trait. As a student, he was respectful and took his academic duties seriously. As a young prince, he remained steadfast in his support of his older brother, the Crown Prince. He had neither the charm nor the ambition to form his own faction. This was how the fourth prince "placed himself in an invincible position".

While the Emperor might have had issues with his chosen successor, he treasured loyalty more than anything else, including loyalty to his chosen heir. By showing allegiance to the Crown Prince during his first fall from grace, the fourth prince passed the loyalty test better than all the other serious contenders for the title.

The fourth prince had another important asset and that was ironically his lack of charm. He was known to be strict; a feature that extended to his tenure as emperor, and that repelled other princes and officials. Kangxi felt safe with him because he was not strong enough to pose any threat. This allowed the fourth prince to position himself in a "place where he cannot be defeated". However, being non-threatening was not the same as being inactive. The fourth prince took every opportunity to demonstrate to his father that he was competent enough to be seriously considered as his successor. He did this without arousing suspicion from the sensitive Kangxi. It was a delicate balancing act.

The Crown Prince was born to succeed the Emperor. However, he lost the title of crown prince not once but twice. Perhaps the special place he once had in Kangxi's heart gave him an inflated sense of self-importance. Perhaps he lacked self-awareness and lost touch with reality because he had surrounded himself with yes men for so long. He fatally misunderstood his father and how he was perceived by his father. This finally led to his downfall. Kangxi had a sensitive and sentimental side that needed to be nurtured. This was totally lost on the Crown Prince. His emotional numbness was interpreted as disloyalty and untrustworthiness. Time and again, he failed to do anything to change his father's perception of him as a constant threat.

The eighth prince was a tragic figure. He had the talents and charisma that would have made him crown prince and emperor if the selection process had been more "democratic". However, what would be an asset in a meritocracy became a liability in a despotic context. In an absolute monarchy, only one vote counted and that was the vote of the Emperor. Having the backing of his brothers and the top officials in the cabinet was seen as a threat by Kangxi and that was the kiss of death for the eighth prince.

From a structural point of view, there's a certain tragic inevitability to what happened to Kangxi's imperial household. Kangxi, taking his cue from the Zhou succession system, named the eldest son of his empress, the second prince Yinreng, as the crown prince.

This seemed to be the perfect case of "While in Rome, do as the Romans do". The problem, however, was that the Manchurian regime, like the Tang Dynasty before it, retained its nomadic characteristics. Unlike the Song and Ming dynasties that adhered strictly to the Zhou succession system by not allowing the princes or even the crown prince to participate in politics for fear of faction-building, the nascent Qing regime gave the sons of the emperor free rein to engage in government affairs.

Always the strategic thinker, Kangxi let his sons hold public offices to balance out the influence of the powerful Aisin-Gioro princes and Manchurian war heroes who had helped Qing unify China. This was not paranoia. While his father had a hard time dealing with his own uncle the prince regent, he himself had to fight to fend off the ego of the chancellor regent who was a formidable Manchurian warrior. Kangxi's own sons could serve as an effective counterweight against these two factions. After all, who could be more reliable than your own sons? But then again, who could be more threatening than your own sons? Kangxi would find out the hard way.

The Emperor wanted the princes to be powerful enough to rein in the Aisin-Gioro noblemen and Manchurian warriors, but not too powerful to threaten his own imperial authority. This, in a nutshell, was the source of conflict between the father and the sons. Take the Crown Prince as an example. Kangxi had great expectations for him and had put him in charge of the government when the he was away for battle. But when his faction became too aggressive in protecting its interests and asserting its authority, it was perceived as a threat to the Emperor. When Kangxi tried to neutralize the threat by raising the status of the other princes, he unwittingly conveyed the impression that the title of crown prince was now up for grabs. As competition for the throne was a zero-sum game, this could only intensify the rivalries among the siblings.

The secret succession system created by Yongzheng was designed to prevent history from repeating itself. Choosing the successor in secret prevented open rivalry and bitter competition that characterized the early Tang and Qing dynasties. During these periods, many members of the royal family perished in their struggle for the title of crown prince. The Song and Ming dynasties followed the uncompetitive Zhou succession system and churned out mediocre emperors. In this aspect, the secret succession system was a marked improvement. Without naming an heir apparent, the system left no room for the development of a crown prince faction or an anti-crown prince faction. Moreover, not only did the system allow for competition among the princes, it enabled the emperor to observe and assess their behavior in secret. Since it was a secret system, the emperor could change his mind any time and no one would know or disapprove. When the emperor made up his mind, his choice would be announced in public after his death. That way, no one could challenge his decision or the legitimacy of his chosen successor.

Fourth Prince Yizhu

Daoguang
【Emperor of Qing】

Yixin
(Sixth Prince)

YIZHU
(Fourth Prince/
Emperor Of Qing)

Chapter 9

What Xianfeng Knew

Dynasty: Qing Dynasty (清)

Period: circa 1840 AD to 1860 AD

Key Players:

The Emperor Daoguang (道光皇帝): Emperor of the Qing Empire who reigned during the forced opening of China by the UK via the First Opium War

The Emperor Xianfeng Yizhu (咸丰皇帝-奕詝): Fourth son of the Emperor Daoguang, kindhearted but mediocre, later became emperor with the title Xianfeng (咸丰皇帝)

Yixin (奕訢): Sixth son of the Emperor Daoguang, intelligent and direct, later Prince Gong (恭亲王) who led the Westernization movement of China

"Thus, it is said if you knew the enemy and yourself, your victory would not be imperiled. If you knew Heaven and Earth, your victory would be complete."

The Art of War, Chapter 10
《知彼知己，胜乃不殆；知天知地，胜乃可全。》
孙子兵法第十章

HISTORICAL CONTEXT

The power transitions that followed Emperor Yongzheng (the fourth prince in Chapter 7) were relatively peaceful as the rulers managed to keep sibling rivalry to a minimum after the bitter conflict that took place in the royal household earlier.[1] Emperor Daoguang began his rule in 1820 AD when both Qing and China reached a turning point.

It was during his reign that the First Opium War was fought. Qing's medieval forces proved no match for the semi-modernized war machine that the British had at their disposal. With its humiliating defeat, the Qing government had to pay twenty-one million silver coins in reparations, cede Hong Kong, and open five ports for trade to the British Empire. Since then, China was forced to open its doors to the dominant foreign powers.

Never before had China been challenged by a technologically superior foreign force. All other conquerors of China prior to the British were barbaric nomads from the north. Initially, the middle kingdom tried to convince itself that the devils from the ocean were its cultural inferiors but found it increasingly difficult to deny the level of scientific advancement and global dominance of the Westerners. The late Qing official that sought to westernize the empire called the period[2] that he lived in "a change in China that she had not witnessed for 3,000 years." By the end of the Opium War, Emperor Daoguang was already over sixty;

---

[1] The transfer of power from him to Qianlong (乾隆) (1735–1796 AD) and then from Qianlong to Jiaqing (嘉庆) (1796–1820 AD) and from Jiaqing to Daoguang (道光) (1820–1850 AD) were without much drama even though they did not follow the strict uncompetitive Zhou succession system that was adhered to during the Song and Ming Dynasties.

[2] The official was Li Hongzhang (李鸿章) who had been instrumental in putting down the Taiping Rebellion (1850–1864 AD). He was at the forefront of the modernization of China but fell into disgrace when his fleet and army were defeated by the Japanese in the Sino-Japanese War (1894–1895 AD). Li Hongzhang would die right after signing the peace treaty with the foreign powers after China's defeat in the Boxer Rebellion.

an age that was considered ancient under the medical circumstances of the time. His heir would have to deal with an existential threat that the Qing Empire and Chinese culture had never faced before.

DEATH OF THE ELDEST PRINCE

Unlike the emperors before him, Daoguang had few children. This could be due to the multi-generational intermarriages between members of the Aisin-Gioro royal household and other Manchu noble families. The Manchu population remained at around two to three million during the Qing dynasty with no more than a few aristocratic families. Such inbreeding no doubt affected the ability of the emperors to produce offspring. It was no accident that the last three emperors of the Qing dynasty were all childless.

Daoguang was quite advanced in years when he had his first son, and the child occupied a special place in his heart as the prince was for a long time the only son he had. Daoguang was known to be one of the most frugal emperors in Chinese history, already having had that habit since he was still a prince. After his status as the heir to the throne became an open secret, he still maintained a very humble lifestyle. Every morning, he would ask his eunuch to go out to the street markets of Beijing and buy five pieces of plain pancakes: two for himself, two for his wife and one for the future first prince.

The education for a Manchurian prince was intense: a Qing emperor once remarked that he coughed up blood due to long periods of intense memorization of Confucian texts. Unlike the princes of other dynasties, Qing princes were required to be adroit in not just Han Chinese and the classics but also Manchurian and Mongolian. Since Qing was a multi-ethnic empire, its emperor was simultaneously the ruler of the Manchus, Hans, Mongolians, Uighurs, and Tibetans. He therefore had to familiarize himself with different cultures and languages and turn himself into "all things to all people".

Moreover, a Manchurian prince had to be adept at archery and horseback riding, the two essential skills that helped the Qing Empire unify China. The royal family attached great importance to the education of its members. Daoguang had great expectations for the first prince who was more likely than others to be chosen as his heir. Unfortunately, the son did not share his father's passion for education. His teacher was understandably distraught over the first prince's cavalier attitude towards his studies.

He admonished the first prince and said, "First prince, you will one day be the Emperor of the Qing Empire, you need to study harder, Your Highness."

To which the first prince replied, "If I ever become the emperor, the first thing I would do is to execute you!"

The first prince's teacher was shocked and related the incident to the Emperor. Like other Manchurian emperors, Daoguang was a strict father. He would have sent a eunuch to beat the first prince, had it not been for the fact that he would do the job better himself. As it happened, he allegedly kicked the first prince in his private parts so hard that the poor boy died three days later.

CHOOSING BETWEEN THE FOURTH AND THE SIXTH PRINCE

With the first prince dead, Daoguang, then in his late sixties, needed to choose an heir out of his three surviving teenage sons: the fourth prince, the fifth prince, and the sixth prince. The fifth prince was out of the running early on. His mother had fallen out of favor with the Emperor and was eventually demoted. He himself was a free spirit and never took his studies seriously. Daoguang became so frustrated with him that he allowed a childless relative to adopt him.

Therefore, it became a race between the fourth prince Yizhu and the sixth prince Yixin. The fourth prince had clear advantages: he was the eldest surviving son, and his mother was from a prominent family which had produced six empresses for the Qing Dynasty, including his mother. However, he was neither eloquent nor physically fit, as was expected of a member of the Manchurian royal family. The sixth prince, in contrast, was not only fluent in the Confucian classics, as required of all Qing princes, but also excelled in horseback riding and archery. He even choreographed his own sabre and spear routines which greatly impressed his father. The sixth prince was also keenly aware of the Western world and would develop a liking for whiskey and cigars later in his life. In short, the heir title was for the fourth prince to lose but Daoguang loved the sixth prince. This pitted the two princes against each other.

The first showdown between the two brothers happened on an uneventful day when Daoguang summoned the two young princes to the Summer Palace. In his residence, the father gave the fourth and sixth princes a choice between a wooden box and a golden box. The fourth prince let the sixth prince choose first and the sixth prince, without hesitation, opted for the golden box. This reflected the personalities of the brothers well.

The fourth prince was kind-hearted with a more subdued personality. The sixth prince was more aggressive: he knew what he wanted and was not afraid to go after it. This episode left a strong impression on Daoguang. He was taken aback by the sixth prince's aggressiveness and was impressed by the fourth prince's humility as well as his willingness to wait his turn.

Daoguang was among the stingiest emperors in Chinese history. No other emperor would have their imperial robes patched up instead of getting new ones for himself or reprimand the eunuchs for paying more than the market price for the patch-up service. None of his consorts were allowed to buy make-up and all had to refrain from wearing silk. The imperial household would only serve meat on festive occasions. In choosing the golden box, the sixth prince demonstrated greed and a desire for material possessions which did not sit well with his father.

Hunting was not merely a hobby for the Manchurian ruling class; it served a number of greater purposes. The Manchurians were a people of hunter-gatherers who organized their military forces in the form of hunting squads. For the royal family, keeping the habit of hunting was a way to pay respect to the roots of the empire. It was also a reminder to the ruling class and the Han officials that Qing was, first and foremost, a Manchurian regime and that the emperor had not forgotten his roots.

Hunting also formed an important part of Manchu princes' education as the imperial household required its offspring to be physically fit. Most emperors of the Qing Dynasty were therefore excellent horsemen and archers. It was customary practice for the emperor to bring his sons along on hunting trips and gave them the opportunity to impress him.

One day in springtime, Daoguang brought his sons to the royal grounds for a hunting session. It was a de facto animal killing competition and the sixth prince won with flying colors. This did not come as a surprise given the physical prowess of the young man. What intrigued the Emperor was the fact that the fourth prince had not pulled the bowstring once during the entire session. He might be physically weak and lame in one leg, but there was no reason for not participating in the game. Then the fourth prince gave his reason: spring is a time for renewal and new beginnings. Hunting at this time would very likely kill new mothers and leave their babies unattended. Heaven has a will to allow things to live; so it is not right to kill in springtime.

Daoguang was extremely impressed by the benevolence of the fourth prince. For him, it was the duty of an emperor to treasure all lives in his domain. Everyone present, not least the sixth prince, was dumbfounded. It was clear that the fourth prince, who lacked the skills to even compete in the hunting match, had used a moral excuse to cover up his athletic incompetence. Be that as it may, it appealed to the Emperor's sense of thrift and benevolence.

Towards the end of his life, Daoguang's health declined rapidly and he knew his days were numbered. He summoned the sixth prince and asked how he would govern the empire if he became its ruler. Before he went to see his father, the sixth prince met with his teacher[3] who urged his student to take this opportunity to demonstrate that he was fit to govern and had what it took to be the next Qing emperor.

The sixth prince took this advice to heart. When he saw the emperor, he gave an eloquent speech on public administration, armed forces, the relationship with "the foreign ghosts from the ocean" (the Westerners) and other important areas of the government. Daoguang was impressed but was also left with a bitter taste in his mouth — the son had clearly figured out what to do after his death. He must have spent a lot of time thinking about gaining power upon his father's passing.

Daoguang talked to the fourth prince as well. Before he left for his father's residence, the fourth prince met with his teacher and received advice that would change the outcome of the succession race and, to a certain extent, the course of Chinese history.

The teacher of the fourth prince knew his student well and had his trust. That meant he could give him his honest opinion and explained to the fourth prince that since he was not nearly as eloquent and competent as his younger brother, he must not try to emulate the sixth prince on discussing policies. Then the teacher told him about how the first prince Cao Pi (Chapter 3) trumped the talent of his brother the third prince Cao Zhi by winning the heart of their father Cao Cao.

As it turned out, the teacher's advice was the fourth prince's ticket to success. By listening to the teacher, the student found a way to his father's heart. The fourth prince went to see his father who asked him the same question — how would you rule the mighty Qing Empire? At that moment, the fourth prince began to weep and said he would rather not have the chance to rule. Daoguang tried to console him but succeeded only in making him cry more uncontrollably. Then the son told the father that he was willing to take a few years out of his life and give them to Daoguang to make him live longer. The father was so moved that he decided to choose the fourth prince as his heir. Heavily influenced by Confucian teaching, the Emperor regarded kindness and filial piety as Qing's moral foundation, and prized order and obedience over progress and competence. In his eyes, the fourth prince was much closer to the ideal of the benevolent ruler than the sixth prince.

---

[3]The teacher of the sixth prince was named Zhuo Bingtian (卓秉恬).

Seen in this light, the race for the throne was just as much between the fourth and the sixth princes as it was between their teachers. The sixth prince's teacher was an accomplished scholar who had joined the Qing bureaucracy by sitting for and excelling in the imperial examination. He rose through the ranks and became a cabinet minister. Politically, he believed that Qing should act more proactively and aggressively to protect its own interests. When he served as the Minister of War, he proposed to strengthen the defense along the areas which were the most vulnerable to the invasion of Western powers.

He was also in favor of combining the Qing forces in a number of southern provinces so as to prevent rebels from taking advantage of administrative boundaries by shuttling between the various jurisdictions to avoid suppression.

The fourth prince's teacher was a different political animal.[4] While he also gained entry to high government office through imperial examinations, he had never held positions that required him to take bold, decisive action like the Minister of War. Belatedly, he took his last, most important imperial examination at thirty-seven. He could not have done so earlier for he had to take care of his father after his mother's death. As a result, he did not enter the government as a scholar until he turned forty. For much of his career, he served as editor in royal libraries and examiner for the imperial examinations. Except for the office of the Minister of Infrastructure, most of the posts the fourth prince's teacher had held were more of an academic than practical nature.

The fourth prince's teacher's style of scholarly meekness and obedience to the Confucian tradition, especially the value of filial piety, had a profound impact on the fourth prince and, as it turned out, suited the Emperor well. During his reign, the fourth prince continued to rely on his teacher. When his teacher died, he wept so hard that everyone who was present also cried. Then he bestowed upon his teacher the highest posthumous honor that had ever been granted to any officials in the Qing regime.[5]

THE EMPEROR, THE BROTHER AND THE CRISIS OF AN EMPIRE

When Daoguang died, the fourth prince succeeded him with the imperial title of Xianfeng. Xianfeng ruled the Qing Empire with his trademark conservatism and

---

[4]The teacher of the fourth prince was named Du Shoutian (杜受田).

[5]The title was "Wenzheng" (文正). Only eight individuals in the Qing Dynasty's entire 268 years of history were given that honor, showing how highly the student regarded his late teacher.

passivity. The sixth prince was given the name Gong from the idiom "*Xiong You Di Gong*" (兄友弟恭) which can be translated as "The older brother should be friendly while the younger brother should be respectful". By granting this title, Xianfeng conveyed a clear message to his brother — I will be friendly, insofar as you remain respectful. The brothers got on well until the mother of the sixth prince passed away.

When Xianfeng went to visit the old consort on her deathbed, the sixth prince proposed naming his mother as empress posthumously. In reply, Xianfeng might have made a sound that the sixth prince construed as the affirmative. Without seeking clarification from the Emperor, the presumptuous sixth prince proceeded to prepare a royal edict ordering the status of his mother be raised to empress. When Xianfeng found out about this, he was furious and accused the sixth prince of falsely communicating the Emperor's wishes, a crime punishable by death. The life of the sixth prince was spared but he was removed from the political center of power.

Xianfeng's Confucian passivity was ill-equipped for the challenges that the Qing Empire was facing at the time. In the 1850s, all of Southern China was ravaged by the Taiping Rebellion, a religious group whose leader believed himself to be the younger brother of Jesus sent to China to rid it of the Manchu devils. At the same time, the French and British were threatening the Qing Empire with modern industrialized weapons and demanding to renew the treaties signed after the First Opium War, which finally led to the Second Opium War. The medieval Qing troops, fighting with bows and arrows, were no match for the European forces. As the French and British forces marched into the capital, Xianfeng left the capital hastily with his Empress, consorts, and his six-year-old son.[6]

The sixth prince, under orders to stay at the capital, saw the Summer Palace being burnt to the ground by the enemy forces. To his eternal shame, he signed the treaty ending the war on behalf of the Qing Empire with the British and the French. The shell-shocked and demoralized Xianfeng spent most of his days drunk. A kind person in sobriety, he would beat the people who attended to him violently when he was intoxicated. Upon regaining consciousness, he would feel guilty and reward the victims handsomely in financial terms. Though the foreign forces had left, he was unwilling to return to the capital, fearing that Beijing was now controlled by his more formidable brother the sixth prince. Before Xianfeng

---

[6]The son's name was Zaichun (载淳). He would succeed Xianfeng to become the Emperor Tongzhi (同治). The Empress Dowager Cixi was his mother.

passed away at the age of thirty and was succeeded by his six-year-old son, he named eight officials as regents[7] to look after the child emperor.

The sixth prince, who was not one of the eight regents, was understandably unhappy with the arrangement. During his brother's reign, he was intentionally sidelined. Then when the foreign forces invaded the capital, he was given the unenviable task of signing the armistice with the ghosts from the ocean. When Xianfeng passed his throne to his infant son, he was excluded from the oligarchy entrusted with the job of running the country. After Xianfeng's death, the eight regents took over the administration and made the mistake of antagonizing the two widows (one of them the formidable Empress Dowager Cixi) of Xianfeng who joined hands with the sixth prince to stage a coup d'état and seized power.[8]

ANALYSIS

"Thus, it is said if you knew the enemy and yourself, your victory would not be imperiled. If you knew Heaven and Earth, your victory would be complete."

The Art of War, Chapter 10

Knowledge holds the key to victory. No one understands this dictum from Sun Tzu better than the fourth prince who completed his victory by knowing Heaven (the heart of his father) and Earth (himself).

Contrary to popular belief, the battle for imperial succession in ancient China was less about sibling rivalry than the mental game between father and son. At the end of the day, it was the father emperor who decided who would qualify as the next emperor. Whether a son could rise or fall, therefore, depended to a great extent on how well he knew himself and his father.

That was the difference between the two princes. Unlike the sixth prince, the fourth prince knew, not only himself but also his father. He knew he was no match for his younger brother in both physical strengths and intellectual abilities, so he avoided direct confrontation with his rival. He knew his father prized benevolence and filial piety over ambition and competence, so he launched into dramatic display of these qualities whenever he had the opportunity to do so.

---

[7] Chief of them was Sushun (肅順), a member of the Aisin-Gioro royal family who was a tough and unpopular leader. One of the eight was Du Han (杜翰) who was the son of Xianfeng's teacher Du Shoutian. Xianfeng was indeed grateful to his teacher and the Emperor's love for him was extended to his son.

[8] Prince Gong would see his career rising and falling while repeatedly partnering and fighting with the Empress Dowager Cixi until his death at the age of 65 in 1898 AD.

If imperial succession was a game, its rules had never been spelled out explicitly. If a player could read the game accurately and understand its implicit rules, he could turn his disadvantages into advantages, and weaknesses into strengths.

The fourth prince's mother was the Empress and he himself was the eldest surviving son. However, the Qing succession process attached little importance to these details. What was far more important was his father's idea of what an emperor should be. If, for example, Daoguang valued the killer instinct and hunting skills more than kindness and empathy, the fourth prince would certainly have lost out to the sixth prince in their competition to impress their father. But it was benevolence that the Emperor treasured. That was not lost on the observant and knowing fourth prince who won the hunting game by refusing to hunt.

Like the first prince Cao Pi from Chapter Three, the fourth prince was another example of the meek inheriting the earth. Approaching the end of his life, Daoguang wanted to be loved and understood more than ever. When the son told him he was willing to make the ultimate sacrifice for him, how could he not be moved? Filial piety is central to Confucianism. By embodying this core value, the fourth prince presented himself as the best possible candidate who, if chosen as successor, would stay the course set by his predecessors. This was in fact what the fourth prince did after ascending to the throne. Whether that was what needed to be done for Qing was another matter.

The good fortune of the fourth prince turned out to be a calamity for the Qing Empire. Daoguang's choice of successor reflected poorly on himself as a ruler. The First Opium War, one of the most momentous events that happened to China, occurred during his reign. Faced with military forces which were technologically far superior, the Qing government should have learnt from its devastating defeat and embarked on a process of modernization. That was what the Japanese did during the Meiji Restoration. There were many reasons for the muted and delayed response of the Qing government, but Daoguang's personality certainly played a key role.

After the First Opium War, Daoguang should have pursued an aggressive policy of transformation for the empire, but the old Emperor instead became even more resistant to change. When a long-serving prime minister[9] retired, his protégé asked him how he could survive having been so close to the apex of power for so long.

The old minister replied, "Speak seldom, kowtow often."

---

[9] The official's name was Cao Zhenyong (曹振镛).

Those four words speak volumes with respect to the leadership style of Daoguang. His thriftiness and conservatism led him to put loyalty and kindness before competence and ability. The fourth prince's behavior therefore matched his idea of a ruler more closely than that of the aggressive sixth prince. By making this over-cautious choice at a time that called for boldness, he doomed the Qing Dynasty.

As for the sixth prince, his loss illustrates another truism in life — character is destiny. He was physically and intellectually superior to his older brother. But his over-confidence and lack of empathy proved to be his undoing. His father wanted his successor to be kind and benevolent. This should have been crystal clear after the hunting trip. But this central fact continued to escape the sixth prince's notice. When he was summoned to the Emperor's deathbed, he took no heed of his father's emotional needs and kept delivering his presentation on the grand schemes that he would launch after inheriting the throne. This lack of empathy remained his defining trait until the end of his life. As the younger brother of Emperor Xianfeng, he mistook his own wishful thinking for the Emperor's approval. This reminds one of how he grabbed the golden box in front of Daoguang many years ago. This type of naked aggression, while useful in certain circumstances, seldom fared well in the court politics of Imperial China.

Chapter 10

Epilogue

THEIR WINNING WAYS — FURTHER THOUGHTS ON THE RISING SON'S STRATEGIES

Upon studying the nine dramatic and representative stories of royal household rivalries in imperial Chinese history, we found that the winners gained the throne very similarly to how leopards hunt their prey in the wild. Leopards are one of the best hunters in the wild and their hunting process broadly follows the following steps:

1) **Observe the target without being exposed** (in fact, leopards are nocturnal predators.)
2) **Maximize the probability of success in stealth mode** by getting as close to it as possible.
3) **Swift Execution:** As and when the timing is right, go for a quick kill and drag the prey up to the tree in order to avoid hyenas.

We shall elaborate the process of gaining the right to becoming heir by drawing the examples from our stories in the space below:

Observe the Target in Hiding

Given that the consequence of showing one's ambition and then failing is death, the target for the royal rivalry game was not simply just to gain the throne. Being the crown prince was one of the most dangerous jobs in ancient China and as such the goal first and foremost was to survive the career of being a prince. As the saying goes, "If you want to finish first, you must first finish." The specific target for a prince should be to maximize the probability of being selected or gaining the throne while minimizing the risk of doing so or as financial professionals like to call it: maximizing the risk-adjusted returns. Since there are so many factors at play, one could not guarantee that one's actions could gain the throne. Rather, the goal should be to stay alive and be in the emperor's good graces and as and when the opportunity would arise, one could be in the position to gain the right of succession. As Sun Tzu said in Chapter 4 of *The Art of War*: "Winning could be known but it could not be forced." The same way, winning in this game requires staying in the game and to seize the opportunity only when it arises.

An example of not being able to manage that risk was Qi Ji (Chapter 2). She made a high-profile attempt to have her husband Liu Bang make their son the third prince Liu Ruyi the crown prince when the Han regime was already determined to follow the Zhou succession system of naming the eldest son of the empress, Liu Ying, to be the heir to the throne. Qi Ji underestimated the political force that was required to change the crown prince that even her husband the emperor Liu Bang did not have at his disposal. Since the Han dynasty was young at the time, Liu Bang was mindful of the political consequences of changing the crown prince. However, by showing her desire to remove the current heir, Qi Ji showed her hand and therefore subjected herself to great danger as soon as her husband died, Crown Prince Liu Ying became the Emperor, and Lü Zhi became the Empress Dowager. Liu Bang himself also violated the principle as his support for appointing the third prince Liu Ruyi as crown prince would subject his favorite consort Qi Ji and his son Liu Ruyi to great danger upon his death. Failure to understand that the objective in court rivalry is to "survive first and strike only when the kill is close" put these individuals in harm's way. Lü Zhi herself also did not understand the principle. She made her nephews vassal kings when her late husband, the founding emperor of the Han Dynasty Liu Bang, had specifically ordered that only members of the Liu clan could be given such positions. The Liu family remained powerful and so did the founding officials of the Han regime; while Lü Zhi did not possess absolute power even though she remained at the helm. By raising her own clan to such a high standing without the necessary political support, she put all of her natal family members in danger. Their quick demise upon her death was in fact a certainty in that political environment. In contrast, Bo Ji and her son the fourth prince Liu Heng understood the principle well. They were able to minimize risk by staying under Lü Zhi's radar and, as and when the opportunity arose, they were in the prime position to gain the highest positions of empress dowager and emperor respectively.

In the Tang dynasty, both the ninth prince Li Zhi and his wife Wu Zetian (Chapter 5) also understood the principle at its core. The ninth prince Li Zhi stayed well clear of the rivalry between his older brothers, but maintained a profile of filial piety throughout his career as the prince. That way he was able to keep his costs to the minimum while his brothers expended their political energies. By simply acting nervous and then seemingly unwillingly telling his father that his fourth brother was threatening him, the ninth prince Li Zhi was able to put the fourth prince out of the race for the crown prince position. With the original crown prince already deposed, the ninth prince Li Zhi was named heir to the throne. The ninth prince Li Zhi's actions reminds one of the Tang poet Du Fu's (杜甫) famous poetic phrase, "The rain comes in with the wind at night, and it moistens everything in silence." (随风潜入夜, 润物细无声。) The ninth prince Li Zhi was indeed like the innocent rain at night. Wu Zetian also had a clear and specific goal and did not expose herself to unnecessary risks in her political career. One of the key policies as she consolidated power while her husband was still alive was not to raise up the members from her natal family. In fact, she exiled them to the barbaric lands in the south during her process of power consolidation. Whatever her motivations, the net effect was that she was identified by the Tang ministerial rank as being fair and impartial. She had a specific goal and that was to gain power and influence. Any personal gain like raising her natal family was only a distraction from her goal. It was only after her power became absolute that she started to put her nephews in key positions, as she was undecided on which side of her family she should choose her heir from. From this perspective, she was more successful than Lü Zhi in Chapter 2. Wu Zetian's natal family in fact fared much better after the old empress' death than Lü Zhi's clan did after her demise, which could be attributed to Wu Zetian's political talent.

Her daughter-in-law Empress Wei wanted to emulate Wu Zetian to become on par with her husband and then take power after his death. It was unfortunate for her and her daughter that she did not assess the situation as well as she should have. Wu Zetian was dominant not just because she was influential with her husband. She also had multiple decades of experience in administration that Empress Wei lacked. Moreover, her husband Li Zhi was the unquestioned ruler of the Tang dynasty while Empress Wei's husband Li Zhe had his brother Li Dan and sister Princess Taiping as powerful Li family members in court. Empress Wei may have had a specific goal to become the next Wu Zetian but she exposed herself too soon. The other predators, namely the Li royal family, came at her when she exposed her ambition. Princess Taiping (Chapter 6) unfortunately did not execute that principle as well as her mother Wu Zetian. When the princess attempted to challenge her nephew in political control, she did not have any specific plans to take over the throne, as far as historical records show. There was no reason to believe she had the plans or the resources to reduce Li Longji to a mere puppet emperor. Her belligerence to her nephew therefore exposed her ambition but she lacked a specific target or plan to gain absolute control. Her behavior was akin to a leopard running around the prey but making no attempts to go for the kill. This would alert not just the target but also other predators around. Princess Taiping was therefore ambushed and killed in a literal sense.

This step reminds one of writing the regular script in Chinese calligraphy, where the character must completely fall within a set box. If the character is a tall one, one has to set the first stroke close to the top of the box. If the character has two or three parts side by side horizontally, one has to set the first stroke very close to the left side. If the character has very few strokes, one has to thicken the strokes in order to balance with the other characters that have more strokes nearby. Therefore, one could conclude that in order to begin the first stroke of a character, the calligrapher must be able to visualize the character beforehand and know where he would place the last stroke. One simply cannot begin without knowing where he wants to end. This goes for household rivalries: if one were to play the game, he or she must know what the end game is supposed to be. Mindful that exposing one's ambition too soon would lead to deadly consequences; the way that the end game should be played was therefore to keep a low profile or lay low, and wait for the perfect opportunity to strike the enemy.

Maximize the Probability of Success in Stealth Mode

Upon identifying the prey, the leopard would seek to move closer to the target and strike in an ambush to maximize the probability of a kill. In the same way, a rivalry or power struggle within a royal household requires the same skill set in order to succeed. Instead of just being passive, a formidable hunter eying the position of successor would attempt to maximize the probability of gaining the throne or being chosen by the father. Remaining patiently in hiding does not mean pure passivity. Much work has to be done, actions that could augment the probability of success closer to one must be carefully identified and taken.

The actions of Lü Buwei in Chapter 1 fit very well with maximizing the probability of success without exposing oneself. Lü Buwei identified that the path of least resistance to putting his man Ying Yiren on the throne was through Lady Huayang, the childless but favorite consort of the Crown Prince of the most powerful state Qin. He succeeded in convincing Lady Huayang that adopting Ying Yiren as her son could secure her future after the death of her elderly husband, the Crown Prince of Qin. Lü Buwei was successful because he was able to align his own interests with the interests of the person he was seeking to convince. Lady Huayang followed the words of Lü Buwei not because it benefited Lü Buwei but because it suited her welfare. That is the art of persuasion at its finest.

The first prince Cao Pi's words and actions in Chapter 3 maximized the probability of him being selected as heir by his father Cao Cao in the least costly way possible. Without overtly demonstrating his talent which he lacked in comparison to his brother the third prince Cao Zhi, and his ambition which he could not have due to his father's dominance, the first prince Cao Pi nonetheless won his father's favor by showing his piety. The most telling scene during the first prince Cao Pi and the third prince Cao Zhi's rivalry was when the third prince Cao Zhi recited the most beautiful piece of literature to praise his father while the first prince Cao Pi merely cried because he was not able to produce a literary piece of the same caliber. Cao Cao himself was a poet but was not moved by the third prince Cao Zhi's first-class piece. Rather, Cao Cao was moved by the first prince Cao Pi's emotional outburst which was the swing factor for him to name the first prince Cao Pi as his heir. The first prince Cao Pi won because he was able to maximize the probability of being named the heir at the lowest cost possible. As psychology would command, the father, as the alpha male and empire builder, would find an aggressive son competitive and unattractive. Consciously, the father may want his heir to be high achieving. However, on a subconscious level, a strong father with a type A personality would most likely prefer a son who is obedient and does not challenge his authority. Therefore, in a situation where the father had complete authority to choose the heir, it was frequently the obedient and meek son who won the race.

Moreover, a father would be more afraid of an overwhelming heir who could cause harm to the other princes. Take the example of Emperor Li Shimin in Chapter 5. Although he was impressed by the talents of the fourth prince, he was taken aback by his aggressive behavior as evidenced by the ninth prince Li Zhi's anxiety during the court rivalry period. At the end of the day, emperors desired harmony in their households and therefore overt aggression from one of the princes would lead the father to believe that there would be bloodshed among his offspring after his death.

Hong Taiji (Chapter 7) succeeded in his bid for the throne because he also was able to maximize his probability of success on a low-cost basis. His father Nurhaci did not explicitly choose an heir but Hong Taiji positioned himself to be the most eligible as his competitors all committed errors which eroded their probability of becoming the master of the regime. His oldest brother fell out of favor very quickly given his aggressiveness to his brothers; an attitude that created a disequilibrium which was abominable to their father Nurhaci. His other elder brother Daisan revealed himself to be greedy for his father's land and also the father's woman which made it difficult for Nurhaci to continue to trust him. Moreover, Daisan mistreated his sons who were powerful and influential in the nascent Qing regime. Manggultai destroyed all his chances with the murder of his own mother. Hong Taiji however was one level above his brothers. He was a competent member in the Manchurian royal family and maintained great relations with his father, his brothers, and more importantly his young nephews. The combination of all these factors led to the consensus to name him the ruler. It was a classic case of making no mistakes and building small wins while minimizing the risk of showing ambition during his princely career that allowed Hong Taiji to be the ultimate winner of the early Qing competition.

The fourth prince Yinzhen (Chapter 8) also became the winner with similar characteristics. The prince was very specific with his goals: he was to minimize his cost of demonstrating any overt ambition by remaining loyal to the original crown prince insofar as the father Kangxi was partial to the first heir. The low-cost approach of the fourth prince Yinzhen allowed him to escape unscathed during the first abolition of the Crown Prince Yinreng which was highly costly to the eighth prince Yinsi. As the last years of Kangxi progressed, the fourth prince Yinzhen was able to maximize the probability of success by staying on the good side of the powerful yet suspicious Kangxi. Like other powerful men, Kangxi abhorred any challenge to his power, be it from the Crown Prince's faction or the eighth prince's. The Crown Prince gathered his support due to his status and that was a threat to his father's security of power. The Manchurian emperors in the early Qing Dynasty were highly insecure: they were from a race of two to three million people attempting to rule over a vast land with a foreign Han population of at least a hundred million. Therefore, Manchu emperors worked harder than their counterparts in other dynasties and were also more sensitive to challenges to their authority. Kangxi therefore tried to raise his own Crown Prince and princes to take part in government so as to counterbalance the challenges to imperial authority from other Manchu aristocratic powers and the Han-dominated bureaucracy. This type of skepticism was not evident in other dynasties ruled by racially

Han emperors like the Song and Ming regimes. However, with the raising of his princes into the core of imperial power, the battleground for power then shifted to Kangxi's own sons. The fourth prince Yinzhen was able to navigate the situation by staying away from the troubled waters. From hindsight, he knew the soft spots of his father and never became a threat to his father's authority. The Crown Prince Yinreng had his own faction which had to be put down by the Emperor himself. The eighth prince Yinsi's popularity led to his own demise. It was only the fourth prince Yinzhen who consistently demonstrated his competence while maintaining a level of isolationism and piety which gave Kangxi comfort that this son of his was talented enough to be emperor and yet unthreatening to himself. The fourth prince Yinzhen was therefore the best example of the stealth approach while maximizing probability of success.

The fourth prince Yizhu (Chapter 9) maximized the probability of being named the heir in a fashion that was similar to that of the first prince Cao Pi (Chapter 3) nearly two millennia before he was born. In fact, the fourth prince Yizhu's course of action was guided by Cao Pi's story, as taught to him by his teacher. History does indeed repeat itself, because people study and learn from history. The fourth prince Yizhu's success stemmed from the fact that either he or his teacher was emphatic of the Emperor Daoguang's sentiments. While not talented physically, the fourth prince Yizhu was able to reframe the rules of the hunting game to a competition of benevolence where he as a weak athlete was instead regarded as a kind individual who found it too violent to kill animals in springtime. This could be regarded as the highest form of maximizing one's gain with the least effort expended. Another area where the fourth prince Yizhu excelled was his ability to emotionally influence his father at a low effort basis. Like Cao Cao in Chapter 3 or indeed all men at the end of their lives, the Emperor Daoguang was more concerned with being cared for as an individual than the future of their vast empire. Cao Cao needed comfort of a weeping son like his eldest son Cao Pi who was worried about his well-being than a literary genius like his third son Cao Zhi. In the same way, the Emperor Daoguang was more affected by the saddened fourth prince Yizhu's display of emotions, than the ambitious and talented sixth prince Yixin. The fourth prince Yizhu therefore won because he was able to be in tune with the sentiments of his father. His maximization of the probability of success was not costly but effective.

Sun Tzu echoed the same principle in Chapter 4 of *The Art of War* where he wrote, "Winners win before they seek battle while losers seek battle before they seek victory." The winners in our stories augmented the game to the point where the circumstances naturally pointed them to be the winners of the rivalries as outlined.

Swift Execution

As and when action was required, the swift execution of the leopard was observed in Chinese imperial history. In the cases where the power was in the father's hands, any swift or drastic action was not necessary or possible as the aim of the game was to have the father emperor choose one of his sons as his successor. In cases where the father was not in absolute control, the drastic and violent action of going for the kill like the leopard would be mandatory. In the cases that we study, the decisive action of the second prince Li Shimin in chapter four would fit with the criterion in this section. By the beginning of the sixth month in 626 AD, the Crown Prince Li Jiancheng and his loyal younger brother the fourth prince Li Yuanji were zeroing in on the second prince Li Shimin and his powerful generals. When the Turks were set to attack the Tang capital, the Crown Prince used the opportunity to draw the second prince Li Shimin's men to follow the fourth prince Li Yuanji for his northern expedition. The second prince Li Shimin himself earned his merit with his vital role in the creation of the Tang Dynasty. His contribution was too stellar for him to keep a low profile, though he continued to go about his business and seek to be in harmony with the Crown Prince. However, as and when it was necessary to act, the second prince Li Shimin did not hesitate and went directly for the necks of the rivals: killing his brothers in the same early morning at the Northern Gate. While the action should not be lauded, from a political struggle perspective, the decisiveness and cleanliness of execution must be recognized. One could make a counterargument that his brothers would not have been any less belligerent against the fourth prince Li Shimin himself.

Li Longji (Chapter 6) exhibited all the aspects of the leopard hunting approach. In his first palace coup d'état, Li Longji was specific with his target to remove Empress Wei. More importantly, he understood that the credit had to be retained to be his own. Therefore, in the onset, he only involved his aunt Princess Taiping rather than his father Li Dan or his older brothers. Without his father or older brothers' involvement, the success of the campaign meant that power had to be allocated to him. The specific target that he set was beneficial for him in the long-term. During his tenure as crown prince and emperor under his father's leadership, he was meek and patient when dealing with his aunt the Princess Taiping. As such, it was the Princess Taiping whose ambition was exposed while there was a lack of a specific objective. Li Longji then seized the opportunity and took down his aunt Princess Taiping and her faction. With the fall of his sister, Li Dan had to turn over his power to his son Li Longji. Li Longji was quiet and peaceful prior to the incident and his coup d'état was as deadly and swift as a leopard's bite onto the prey's neck. This is consistent with the way a leopard would hunt by only showing itself at the moment of attack. Human action after all must be benchmarked to nature, where we belong.

Appendix 1

Overview of the Succession Process in Ancient China

How was the successor of an empire selected? That was the paramount question for all regimes across history. In Chinese history, the heir of the throne was called the "foundation of the nation" (国本) as he represented the future of the regime. Understanding how the heir was chosen in ancient times allows one to gain profound insight into the history of a particular culture. The topic is specifically interesting in Chinese history due to its repeated cycles of unified dynasties and warring disunities. As time went by, founders of a new unified dynasty would learn from the mistakes of previous regimes. A key area that were continuously updated was the hereditary structure of imperial power. That was the very foundation of the empire!

Chinese history is a complicated subject with a myriad of dates, names, and facts. It is difficult to understand it in its entirety. The purpose of this text is to use a common theme throughout Chinese history which is dramatic, interesting, and useful for the Western reader. Out of the themes within Chinese history, the issue of monarchical succession is one of the most intriguing and educational. Royal family rivalries seeking to be selected as heir was the most dangerous game that one could engage in; either you win and gain the entire domain under the heaven or you lose and your life is in danger. As such, observing Chinese history through the bitterest struggles to be heir to the throne allows the reader to see human behavior at its most intense state given the stakes involved.

THE CORE SUCCESSION SYSTEM

We start with the Western Zhou dynasty (西周) from 1046 BC when it unified the areas in modern day central China where Chinese culture was mainly situated. The previous dynasties of Xia (夏) and Shang (商) left few written records for us to perform a thorough analysis. The Zhou system, on which Confucianism was based, emphasized on ORDER. The Zhou regime was ruled by the Zhou King whose legitimacy was bestowed from above as he was proclaimed as the "Son of Heaven" (天子). The Zhou King would rule metaphorically in the "center" and the lands surrounding the Zhou King were granted to vassal chiefs according to their closeness in blood to the king or the laurels they earned during Zhou's unification campaign. The Zhou regime created "The Rites of Zhou" (周礼), a system to maintain strict ORDER within and between each echelon of the nobles. A certain rank meant you could dress in a certain way or the number of horse chariots you could maintain in your state's army.

With Zhou's obsession with ORDER, it was only natural that they would create a succession system to maintain the ranks through the generations. This system would be a reference for almost all the dynasties that came after the Zhou. The Zhou system was paternal, meaning that the king would pass his throne to his son and a duke would pass his title to his son and so on. The key question is which son would be able to assume power. The Zhou succession system was simple with eight Chinese characters: *li di, li zhang, li xian, li ai* (立嫡, 立长, 立贤, 立爱). The translation meant that the throne, according to this system, would be passed down in this order: The first choice would be the eldest son of the queen; if the queen did not have any sons, the eldest son would be next in line. If there were any issues with the oldest son or there were special circumstances, then the most virtuous son would assume the throne. The last and worst form would be to choose the heir according to the personal love the father had for a particular son. This implied an utter disregard for objective circumstances and the ruler merely selected the foundation for the future of the regime according to his own emotions. One could clearly see that the Zhou's hereditary system placed more emphasis on order than on progress. The status of the heir was known at birth and therefore no competition was necessary or allowed.

It is important to note that there is a common misconception that powerful men in ancient China had multiple wives. In fact, it is more accurate to state that men in the past had one wife and multiple consorts or concubines. The legal status of the wife and her sons with the father had a different legal status from those who were born from a consort. The character *di* (嫡) can be split to two parts: the left side *nü* (女) means woman and the right side *di* (商) means the stem or the base. The main wife (嫡) was the stem of the family and her oldest son was the *dizhangzi* (嫡长子), who was the eldest from the stem. Commonly, the main wife of a noblemen would be from another powerful family and so the eldest son from the main wife would also have relations with other vassal states via his mother. Concubines would tend to be of lower birth and as such their sons would not be as well-endowed politically. This priority system ensured maximum order as this limited sibling rivalry and also maintained a tight grid by blood among the aristocracy.

However, there would be circumstances where the king would prefer a son who was not the oldest from the main wife. It could be because of the son's own talents and power in court or because the king had a particular fondness for the son's mother, who was a concubine. These situations tended to create court rivalries.

BRIEF HISTORY OF SUCCESSION

The Zhou regime descended into chaos despite its best efforts and China disintegrated during the Spring and Autumn Period (770–476 BC) (春秋) and Warring States Period (476–221 BC) (战国). China entered into the imperial age when the First Emperor Qin Shihuang (秦始皇) conquered the other warring states and put China under a central administration rather than allowing his relatives to be vassal kings in 221 BC. There were other dynasties where there were vassal states but the norm for all imperial governments was to govern the whole country from the center. However, Qin Shihuang's Qin Dynasty (秦) proved to be short-lived and China was unified under the Han Dynasty (汉) in 202 BC. Qin Shihuang did not create a new succession system for the pioneering imperial order and his lack of clarity in identifying his heir was one of the key reasons for the demise of his dynasty.

The Han Dynasty mostly followed the Zhou succession system of passing the throne to the eldest son of the empress with a few dramatic exceptions. Since many emperors died young, a lot of the successors where chosen by powerful officials as their puppets. China then descended into disunity during most of the period from "The Yellow Turban Rebellion" (黄巾之乱) in 184 AD to the unification of the Sui Dynasty (隋) in 589 AD. The period would be known as "the Wei-Jin and Northern and Southern Dynasties" (魏晋南北). The Sui Dynasty was short lived (581–618 AD) and was replaced by the mighty Tang Dynasty (唐) (618–906 AD). Both the Sui and Tang Dynasty royal families came from the Northern Dynasties which were established by nomads from the Mongolian steppes. While they followed the Zhou succession system, they nonetheless retained certain nomadic family characteristics. The northern nomads would have the whole family hunt together and therefore there was competition between brothers. Given the lack of human capital, they could not afford the luxury of dividing the statuses between sons. They all had to take their bow and arrow, ride their horses, and fight the enemy. Another important characteristic is the high status of women in the family. The first 137 years of the Tang Dynasty from 618 AD to 755 AD were arguably the most glorious years of imperial China. The boundaries of the empire stretched as far as central Asia and culturally, China's neighbors saw the middle kingdom as the center of civilization. Ironically or maybe casually, every single succession during that period from the founding Tang Emperor Li Yuan's (Chapter 4) abdication in 629 AD to Li Longji's (Chapter 6) assumption of absolute power in 713 AD involved some form of violent rivalry. Even though the Tang Emperors wished to follow the Zhou succession system, the nomadic nature of competition among siblings and powerful women in the household meant for a cut-throat era for the royal Li household. This could be called "The Zhou Succession System with Nomadic Characteristics." During that period, the empresses, princes, and princesses were all involved in the palace rivalries. While the feuds would have caused the Zhou Kings to cringe, the competition that stemmed from them also meant that the ones in power during the period were strong and aggressive. Here lies one of the most difficult issues to balance for any leader deciding on the future of his regime: a well-structured order meant peace, but peace meant a lack of training of the will to expand. One would observe the imperial succession system to flip back and forth between these two conflicting realities.

China fell into disunity again with the "An Lushan Rebellion" (安史之乱) in 755 AD, and although it was officially subdued in 763 AD, China remained divided by regional warlords until the end of the Tang Dynasty in 906 AD. The country continued to be divided during the "Five Dynasties, Ten Kingdoms" (五代十国) era and would be partially reunified again by Song Taizu Zhao Kuangyin (宋太祖赵匡胤), the first emperor of the Song Dynasty (宋) in 960 AD. Having observed the chaos that happened in the previous 200 years, the designers of the political structure of the Song regime reverted to the Zhou or Confucian belief that order should trump all else. As such, Confucianism would be exalted to a level like never before. Consistent with its desire for maintaining order, the Song Dynasty followed a very strict Zhou succession system of passing the throne to the oldest son of the Empress. The Song Dynasty would experience the most peaceful transitions in power than any other Chinese dynasty. Apart from the suspicious circumstances under which its first emperor Zhao Kuangyin died in

976 AD, there were hardly any cases of long-term violent rivalries in the Song court. More importantly, unlike the Tang Dynasty where all the princes participated in politics, the other sons of the emperor remained in the capital city but were kept away from politics. For example, Song Huizong Zhao Ji (宋徽宗赵佶) became emperor in 1100 AD when his brother, the previous emperor, died without a son. Prior to assuming the throne, Zhao Ji spent his days painting and playing ancient soccer. He excelled at both but unfortunately for Song China and himself, his talents did not extend to being a leader. Northern Song would fall completely due to his misdeeds. By excluding princes from government, they were not able to build their power bases like the ones in the Tang dynasty did. On the flip side, the Song emperors were mostly passive and inexperienced men that lacked the aggression and willpower of the early Tang rulers. The Song dynasty therefore exchanged expansionism for peace at court.

The Yuan Dynasty (元) would unite China in 1278 AD. The Mongolians never seriously adopted the core Confucian culture of the Han Chinese and their succession system reflected this. Nearly each transition in power was through some form of open and violent rivalry without any systematic mechanism. The Ming Dynasty (明) followed with its first emperor Ming Taizu Zhu Yuanzhang (明太祖朱元璋) assuming the throne in 1368 AD. The Ming emperors ruled with a tighter fist than their Song counterparts, but they nonetheless adhered strictly to the Zhou succession system. Apart from the exceptional cases of "The Jingnan Rebellion" (靖难之变) from 1399 to 1402 AD and "The Tumu Crisis" (土木堡之变) in 1449 AD where military campaigns were involved, all the other transitions in power were peaceful.

One example could illustrate the Ming regime's respect for the Zhou succession system. Ming Shenzong Zhu Yijun (明神宗朱翊钧) who ruled from 1573 to 1620 AD was the longest reigning emperor in the Ming Dynasty. He was not particularly fond of his wife and as a result they did not have children together. On a certain day, the Emperor went to pay respects to his mother and while waiting for her, he copulated with a court lady who was cleaning the room at the time. The court lady then gave birth to his eldest son. However, despite the arrival of a male royal child, the Emperor was neither fond of the court lady nor their child. Instead, he was in love with another consort and they had a son together, the third prince. The Emperor desired to have the third prince as his heir but the government bureaucracy would not allow for it. The first prince was the eldest son and since the Empress had no child, he was naturally the rightful heir. The third prince was neither the eldest nor a child from the empress; so there was no basis to make him the crown prince. The Emperor even protested to the bureaucracy by not attending official court meetings for twenty years. However, the Zhou succession system was so ingrained in the Ming regime that even the Emperor's strike could not change the reality. The oldest son would eventually assume the throne when his father died. A fully functioning Zhou succession system was more than just a strict adherence to the order of preference for the heir. It was also needed to inhibit the political influence of the other princes in order to eliminate any potential competition. The Ming princes were made vassal kings, but they were effectively prisoners in their own regional palaces. Communication with the capital in Beijing was strictly forbidden and they had no administrative power in their own vassal domains. As such, nearly no Ming prince ever became influential enough to challenge the Zhou succession system. The Ming regime also was very inward looking and therefore, like the Song Dynasty, they emphasised harmony at court over expanding the empire.

The last dynasty of imperial China was the Qing Dynasty which was a regime founded by the Manchurian leader Nurhaci. A nomadic tribe in its origin, the Manchu race nonetheless was closer to Han culture than the Mongolians who founded the Yuan Dynasty. When the Qing government entered into the Han region of China in 1644 AD, the regime would inherit the Ming system of Confucian bureaucracy while reserving the top positions of government for the Manchurian noblemen. The desire to create an integrated empire while simultaneously maintaining the tradition of military involvement for princes meant that there were bitter rivalries in the succession process in the Qing regime in its early days. From the death of Nurhaci in 1626 AD to the assumption of the throne by Emperor Yongzheng (the fourth prince Yinzhen in Chapter 8) in 1722 AD, every transition in power involved some form of intense court rivalry. One could draw similarities between early Qing with the early Tang where the regime was run with a keen desire to follow Zhou principles of maintaining order while preserving elements of a competitive nomadic spirit. Just like the Tang dynasty earlier, early Qing was one of the most expansive and successful empires that Chinese history had ever seen. Again, there was a negative relationship between order in court and territorial expansion of a regime.

The Emperor Yongzheng, having experienced one of the most bitter court rivalries, eventually created a "secretive succession system" which blended the Zhou succession structure with elements of competition and training. The emperor would, towards the end of his life, write down the name of his chosen heir and put the document behind the plaque hanging from the ceiling in the "Palace of Heavenly Purity" (乾清宮) in the Forbidden City. When the emperor died, a eunuch would take the document and read out the name of the heir for all to know. The purpose of the system was to maintain the balance between competition and harmony. A strict Zhou succession system lacked meritocracy and training for the future rulers. With competition, the chance of family rivalry was high. This way, the princes could compete under the supervision of the father. When the father died, the heir would assume absolute power and so all competition would have to cease. The system seemed to work as the succession processes of the next generations were smooth and the competitive process allowed the future emperors to have experience in government. After the death of the Emperor Xianfeng (the fourth prince Yizhu in Chapter 9) in 1861 AD, the Qing emperors who assumed the throne were all infants and were childless upon their deaths. The system was therefore rendered useless. Since the Qing was the last dynasty in Chinese history, one would not be able to observe if this system could stand the test of time.

Appendix 2

Selection Criteria
for the Rising Sons

The selection of the main characters in the book was made as objectively as historical analysis could allow, so that one would not fall into the trap of espousing a theory and then cherry-picking data to support it.

The method by which "the rising sons" were chosen is outlined as follows: China went through periods of unification and division and the understanding of how the throne was passed is valuable insofar as the regime was a unified or at least dominant government that ruled within the borders of modern-day China. We define dominant regime as one ruling at least 60% of the known population at the time of that regime within the modern boundaries of the People's Republic of China. The data starts from the eve of the Qin Dynasty when the First Emperor united the most populated parts of China through to the end of the Qing Dynasty. The attached table lists the regimes that fit with the aforementioned criteria of the dominant government within the borders of modern-day China in its era. Since the most populated areas are the Han-dominated provinces that are located in the Eastern part of China, most of these regimes identified themselves as the Middle Kingdom that were predominantly racially Han and followed the Confucian political philosophy.

Throughout history, within the dominant regimes, there were 109 transitions in power. We have broadly categorized these transitions into the following six ways (see Table 1):

Table 1:   Power Transition in Imperial China

秦 (Qin)	Code	*汉宣帝刘询 Liu Xun	B	汉桓帝刘志 Liu Zhi	B
秦孝文王嬴柱 Ying Zhu		汉元帝刘奭 Liu Shi	A	汉灵帝刘宏 Liu Hong	B
亲庄襄王嬴异人 (Ch1 Ying Yiren)	C	汉成帝刘骜 Liu Ao	A	汉少帝刘辩 Liu Bian	B
秦始皇嬴政 Ying Zheng	B	汉哀帝刘欣 Liu Xin	A	汉献帝刘协 Liu Xie	B
秦二世胡亥 Ying Huhai	D	汉平帝刘衎 Liu Kan	B	**魏 (Wei)**	**Code**
秦三世子婴 Yíng Ziying	B	汉孺子刘婴 Liu Ying	B	魏武帝曹操 Cao Cao	
西汉 **(Western Han)**	**Code**	东汉 **(Eastern Han)**	**Code**	魏文帝曹丕 (Ch3 Cao Pi)	C
汉高祖刘邦 Liu Bang		光武帝刘秀 Liu Xiu		魏明帝曹叡 Cao Rui	A
汉惠帝刘盈 Liu Ying	A	汉明帝刘庄 Liu Zhuang	A	魏哀帝曹芳 Cao Fang	B
汉少帝刘恭 Liu Gong	B	汉章帝刘炟 Liu Da	A	魏废帝曹髦 Cao Mao	B
汉少帝刘弘 Liu Hong	B	汉和帝刘肇 Liu Zhao	B	魏元帝曹奂 Cao Huan	B
汉文帝刘恒 (Ch2 Liu Heng)	C	汉殇帝刘隆 Liu Long	B	西晋 **(Western Jin)**	**Code**
汉景帝刘启 Liu Qi	A	汉安帝刘祜 Liu Hu	B	武帝司马炎 Sima Yan	
七王之乱 Rebellion of the Seven States	W	汉少帝刘懿 Liu Yi	B	惠帝司马衷 Sima Zhong	A
汉武帝刘彻 Liu Che	A	汉顺帝刘保 Liu Bao	B	八王之乱 War of the Eight Princes	W
汉昭帝刘弗陵 Liu Fuling	B	汉冲帝刘炳 Liu Bing	B	怀帝司马炽 Sima Chi	B
汉废帝刘贺 Liu He	B	汉质帝刘缵 Liu Zuan	B	愍帝司马邺 Sima Ye	B

Table 1: *(Continued)*

隋 (Sui)	Code	唐顺宗李诵 Li Song	A	宋仁宗赵祯 Zhao Zhen	A
隋文帝杨坚 Yang Jian		唐宪宗李纯 Li Chun	A	宋英宗赵曙 Zhao Shu	A
隋炀帝杨广 Yang Guang	C	唐穆宗李恒 Li Heng	A	宋神宗赵顼 Zhao Xu	A
隋恭帝杨侑 Yang Yiou	B	唐敬宗李湛 Li Zhan	A	宋哲宗赵煦 Zhao Xu	A
唐 (Tang)	Code	唐文宗李昂 Li Ang	B	宋徽宗赵佶 Zhao Ji	A
唐高祖李渊 Li Yuan		唐武宗李炎 Li Yan	B	宋钦宗赵桓 Zhao Huan	A
唐太宗李世民 (Ch4 Li Shi Min)	D	唐宣宗李忱 Li Chen	B	元 (Yuan)	Code
唐高宗李治 (Ch5 Li Zhi)	C	唐懿宗李漼 Li Cui	B	元世祖忽必烈 Kublai	
唐中宗李显 Li Xian	B	唐僖宗李儇 Li Xuan	B	元成宗鐵穆耳 Timur	F
唐睿宗李旦 Li Dan	B	唐昭宗李晔 Li Ye	B	元武宗海山 Qayshan	F
武则天 Wu Zetian	C	唐德宗李适 Li Gua	A	元仁宗愛育黎拔力 八達 Ayurparibhadra	F
唐中宗李显 Li Xian	D	唐顺宗李诵 Li Song	A	元英宗硕德八剌 Suddhipala	F
唐睿宗李旦 Li Dan	D	唐哀帝李柷 Li Zhu	B	也孙铁木儿 Yesün-Temür	F
唐玄宗李隆基 (Ch6 Li Long Ji)	D	北宋 (Northern Song)	Code	元天順帝阿速吉八 Arigaba	F
唐肃宗李亨 Li Heng	E	宋太祖赵匡胤 Zhao Kuangyin		元文宗圖帖睦爾 Toq-Temür	F
唐代宗李豫 Li Yu	A	宋太宗赵光义 Zhao Guangyi	D	元明宗和世剌 Qoshila	F
唐德宗李适 Li Gua	A	宋真宗赵恒 Zhao Heng	A	元文宗圖帖睦爾 Toq-Temür	F

(Continued)

Table 1: (*Continued*)

				清 (Qing)	Code
元宁宗懿璘質班 Irinchibal	F	明孝宗朱佑樘 Zhu Youcheng	A	清太祖努尔哈赤 Nurhaci	
元惠宗妥懽貼睦爾 Toghan Temur	F	明武宗朱厚照 Zhu Houzhao	A	清太宗皇太极 (Ch7 Hong Taiji)	C
明 (Ming)	**Code**	明世宗朱厚熜 Zhu Houcong	A	清世祖福临 Fulin	B
明太祖朱元璋 Zhu Yuanzhang		明穆宗朱载垕 Zhu Zaihou	A	清圣祖玄烨 Xuanye	B
明惠帝朱允炆 Zhu Yunwen	A	明神宗朱翊钧 Zhu Yijun	A	清世宗胤禛 (Ch8 Yinzhen)	C
靖难之变 Jingnan Campaign	W	明光宗朱常洛 Zhu Changluo	A	清高宗弘历 Hongli	A
明成祖朱棣 Zhu Di	E	明熹宗朱由校 Zhu Youjiao	A	清仁宗颙琰 Yongyan	A
明仁宗朱高炽 Zhu Gaochi	A	明思宗朱由检 Zhu Youjian	A	清宣宗旻宁 Minning	A
明宣宗朱瞻基 Zhu Zhanji	A			清文宗奕詝 (Ch9 Yi Zhu)	C
明英宗朱祁镇 Zhu Qizhen	A			清穆宗载淳 Zaichun	B
明代宗朱祁钰 Zhu Qiyu	E			清德宗载湉 Zaitian	B
明英宗朱祁镇 Zhu Qizhen	D			末代皇帝溥仪 Puyi	B
明宪宗朱见深 Zhu Jianshen	A				

Method A: The adult lawful successor assumed the throne with little or no competition, which accounted for 39 transitions.

Method B: A child or a powerless adult succeeded the throne or was installed by a powerful external force; implying that the individual did not take part in gaining the ruling position. This method accounted for 40 power transitions.

Method C: An adult prince who successfully competed for the throne and won through shrewd political moves. This accounted for nine power transitions.

Method D: An adult prince who successful competed and gained power by staging violent coup d'états or court violence. This accounted for seven power transitions.

Method E: A successor gained the throne due to war time circumstances. This accounted for three transitions.

Method F: This is reserved specifically for the Mongolian Yuan Dynasty where the throne was up for competition within the royal Mongolian Borjigit family in a violent matter. This accounted for 11 transitions.

Included in the table are sibling wars (W) which happened when princes were given domains at the geographical fringe of the empire and they would rebel and wage war against the central imperial court.

SELECTING THE STORIES FOR THIS TEXT

The intention of this book is to allow readers to observe Chinese history through the common and dramatic thread of royal household rivalries in power transitions that could provide educational value in terms of what led to successes and failures. The stories that are chosen ought to fit with the following criteria:

1) There were enough twists and turns to provide enough information for the characters involved in the story; i.e. the historical case was dramatic and exciting. This would leave out all the proper non-competing as well as the puppet power transitions as defined by methods A and B.
2) The rivalry was a battle of wits rather than pure violence which compels us to leave out the war time transitions as defined by method E as well as Yuan dynasty power successions as represented by method F.

As such, we have selected nine stories in Chinese history: seven transitions in power as defined by method C and two cases categorized as method D which we believe to be the most representative of court rivalries. Moreover, the historical characters involved in the stories were truly impactful in setting the course of Chinese history. As discussed in the overview of the succession process, the early Tang (618–712 AD) and early Qing (1626–1722 AD) were the periods of the "Zhou Succession System with Nomadic characteristics" in their hereditary structure which was where our stories were clustered.

Bibliography

CHAPTER 1: YING YIREN

Bielenstein, Hans. *The Bureaucracy of Han Times*. Cambridge: Cambridge University Press, 1980.

Chen, Qiyo 陳奇猷 ed. *Lüshi chunqiu xin jiaoshi* 呂氏春秋新校釋 *[Master Lü's Spring and Autumn Annals]*, Shanghai: Shanghai Gunji Chubanshe [Shanghai Chinese Classics Publishing House] 2002.

Crump, J. I. "How the merchant Lu Pu-wei invested in a king's son and became a great minister". In *Strategies of Qin in Chan-Kuo Tśe*. Oxford: Clarendon Press, 1970.

Fu, Sinian 傅斯年. *Zhanguo zijia xulun* 戰國子家敍論. rpt, Shanghai: Shanghai Guji Chubanshe [Shanghai Chinese Classics Publishing House], 2012.

Gu, Yanwu 顧炎武, and Huang Rucheng 黃如成 ed. *Rizhi lu jishi* 日知錄集釋. Changsha: Yuelu Publishing House, 1994.

He, Ning 何寧 ed. *Huainanzi jishi* 淮南子集釋. Beijing: Zhonghua Book Company, 1998.

Jingmenshi Bowuguan 荊門市博物館. *Guodian Chu mu zhujian* 郭店楚墓竹簡. Beijing: Wenwu, 1998.

Kang, Youwei 康有為. *Xinxue wei jing kao* 新學偽經考. 1891, rpt. Beijing: Zhonghua Book Company, 1956.

Knoblock, John, and Jeffrey Riegel. *The Annals of Lü Buwei* 呂氏春秋. California: Stanford University Press, 1999.

Lin, Jianming 林劍鳴, Shi Gao Qin 秦史稿. Shanghai: Shanghai Renmin Meishu Chubanshe [Shanghai People's Fine Arts Publishing House], 1981.

Liu, Xiang 劉向. *Zhanguo ce* 戰國策. Shanghai: Shanghai Guji Chubanshe [Shanghai Chinese Classics Publishing House], 1995.

Loewe, Michael, and Edward L. Shaughnessy, *The Cambridge History of Ancient China: from the Origins of Civilization to 221 B.C.* Cambridge: Cambridge University Press, 2007.

Loewe, Michael. *The Government of the Qin and Han Empires: 221 BCE–220 CE*. Indianapolis: Hackett Publishing Company, 2006.

Ma, Duanlin 馬端臨. *Wenxian tongkao* 文獻通考. Shanghai: Commercial Press, 1936.

Ruan, Yuan 阮元 ed. *Shisan jing zhushu* 十三經注疏. Beijing: Zhonghua Book Company, 1991.

Sawyer, Ralph D. *Sun-tzu The Art of War in Translation*. New York: Barnes & noble, 1994.

Sima, Guang 司馬光. *Zizhi Tongjian* 資治通鑑. Shanghai: Shanghai Shudian, 1989.

Sima, Qian. "Biography of Lord Shang". In *Records of the Grand Historian of China*. New York: Columbia University Press, 1962.

Sima, Qian. "Annals of Qin Shi Huang". In *Records of the Grand Historian of China*. New York: Columbia University Press, 1962.

Sima, Qian. "Biography of Master Lü Buwei". In *Records of the Grand Historian of China*. New York: Columbia University Press, 1962.

Sima, Qian. "Biography of Lord Chunshen". In *Records of the Grand Historian of China*. New York: Columbia University Press, 1962.

Sima, Qian 司馬遷. *Shi ji* 史記. Beijing: Zhonghua Book Company, 1963.

Wang, Xianqian 王先謙. *Han shu buzhu* 漢書補注. Beijing: Zhonghua Book Company, 1983.

Yan, Gengwang 嚴耕望. *Zhongguo difang xingzheng zhidu shi* 中國地方行政制度史. Taipei: Institute of History and Philology, 1961.

Yang, Bing'an 楊丙安 ed. *Shiyi jia zhu Sunzi jiaoli* 十一家注孫子校理. Beijing: Zhonghua Book Company, 1999.

Zhang, Jinguang 張金光. *Qin zhi yanjiu* 秦制研究. Shanghai: Shanghai Guji Chubanshe [Shanghai Chinese Classics Publishing House], 2004.

Zhang, Jue 張覺 ed. *Wu Yue chunqiu jiaozheng zhushu* 吳越春秋校證注疏. Beijing: Intellectual Property Publishing House Co., 2014.

Zhang, Jue 張覺 ed. *Han Feizi jiaoshu* 韓非子校疏. Shanghai: Shanghai Guji Chubanshe [Shanghai Chinese Classics Publishing House], 2010.

Zheng, Liangshu 鄭良樹. *Shang Yang ji qi xuepai* 商鞅及其學派. Shanghai: Shanghai Guji Chubanshe [Shanghai Chinese Classics Publishing House], 1989.

Zhu, Zugeng 諸祖耿 ed. *Zhanguo ce jizhu huikao* 戰國策集注匯考. Rev. ed. Nanjing: Fenghuang Chubanshe, 2008.

CHAPTER 2: LIU HENG

Ban, Gu 班固. *Han shu* 漢書. 32–92. Beijing: Zhonghua Book Company, 1962.

Bielenstein, Hans. *The Bureaucracy of Han Times.* New York: Cambridge University Press, 1980.

Chen, Zhi 陳直. *Han shu xin zheng* 漢書新証. 2nd ed. Tianjin: Renmin chubanshe, 1979.

Cheng, Shude 程樹德. *Jiuchao lu kao* 九朝律考. Beijing: Zhonghua shuju, 1963.

Ch'u, T'ung-tsu, and Jack L. Dull ed. *Han Social Structure.* Seattle: University of Washington Press, 1972.

Duan, Chengshi 段成式. *Youyang Zazu* 酉陽雜俎. Beijing: Xueyuan Chubanshe, 2001.

Dubs, H. H. (compiled by Rafe De Crespigny). *Official Titles of the Former Han Dynasty.* Centre of Oriental Studies in Association with Australian National University Press, 1967.

Ebrey, Patricia Buckley. *The Aristocratic Families of Early Imperial China: A Case study of the Po-ling Tsui Family.* Cambridge: New York: Cambridge University Press, 1978.

Gu, Yanwu 顧炎武, Huang Rucheng 黃如成 ed. *Rizhi lu jishi* 日知錄集釋. Changsha: Yuelu, 1994.

Hsu, Cho-yun. *Ancient China in Transition: An Analysis of Social Mobility,* 722–222 B.C. Calif., Stanford University Press, 1965.

Hsu, Cho-yun. *Han Agriculture: The Formation of Early Chinese Agrarian Economy (206 B.C.–A.D. 220).* London: University of Washington Press, 1980.

Kang, Youwei 康有為. *Xinxue wei jing kao* 新學偽經考. 1891, rpt. Beijing: Guji, 1956.

Lai, Ming-Chiu. "Inheritance Custom in the Han Dynasty". *A Journal of the History Department Society* 9 (1995): 1–20. Hong Kong: New Asia College.

Lai, Ming-Chiu, "Legitimation of Qin-Han China: From the Perspective of the Feng and Shan Sacrifices (206 B.C.–A.D. 220)". In *The Legitimation of New Orders: Case Studies in World History*, edited by Yuen-sang Leung, 1–26. Hong Kong: The Chinese University Press, 2007.

Lai, Ming-Chiu. *Power Convergence and Social Order: The Study of Local Society of the Han Empire* 輻輳與秩序：漢帝國地方社會研究. Hong Kong: The Chinese University of Hong Kong Press, 2013.

Liu, An 劉安. edited and translated by John S. Major, Sarah A. Queen, Andrew Seth Meyer, and Harold D., Roth. *The Huainanzi* 淮南子. New York: Columbia University Press, 2010.

Loewe, Michael. *Bing from Farmer's Son to Magistrate in Han China.* Cambridge: Hackett Publishing, 2011.

Loewe, Michael. *Chinese Ideas of Life and Death: Faith, Myth and Reason in the Han Period (202 BC–220 AD.* London: Routledge & CRC Press, 2018.

Loewe, Michael. *Crisis and Conflict in Han China, 104 B.C.–9 A.D.* London: Allen & Unwin, 1974.

Loewe, Michael. *Divination, Mythology and Monarchy in Han China.* Cambridge: Cambridge University Press, 1994.

Loewe, Michael. *Dong Zhongshu, a "Confucian" Heritage and the Chunqiu Fanlu.* Leiden: Brill, 2011.

Loewe, Michael. *Everyday Life in Early Imperial China during the Han Period, 202 BC–220 AD.* London: Batsford, 1968.

Loewe, Michael, and Edward L. Shaughnessy. *The Cambridge History of Ancient China: from the Origins of Civilization to 221 B.C.* Cambridge: Cambridge University Press, 2007.

Loewe, Michael. *The Government of the Qin and Han Empires: 221 BC–220 AD.* Hackett Pub. Co., 2006.

Loewe, Michael. *The Men Who Governed Han and Xin Periods.* Leiden; Boston: Brill, 2004.

Ma, Duanlin 馬端臨. *Wenxian tongkao* 文獻通考. Shanghai: Commercial Press, 1936.

Mills, Charles Wright. *The Sociological Imagination.* New York: Oxford University Press, 1959.

Pan, Ku. *The History of the Former Han Dynasty* 前漢書: *A Critical Translation with Annotations by Homer H. Dubs.* Baltimore: Waverly Press, 1938.

Ropp, Paul S. *Heritage of China: Contemporary Perspective on Chinese Civilization.* Berkeley: University of California Press, 1990.

Ruan, Yuan 阮元 ed. *Shisan jing zhushu* 十三經注疏. Beijing: Zhonghua Book Company, 1991.

Sawyer, Ralph D. *Sun-tzu The Art of War in Translation.* New York: Barnes & Noble, 1994.

Schmidt-Glintzer, Helwig. "The Scholar-Official and his Community: The Character of the Aristocracy in Medieval China." *Early Medieval China* 1 (1994). 60–83.

Sima, Guang. *Zizhi Tongjian* 資治通鑑. Shanghai: Shanghai Shudian, 1989.

Tanigawa, Michio. *Medieval Chinese Society and the Local Community.* Translated by Joshua A. Fogel. Berkeley; Los Angeles; London: University of California Press, 1985.

Wang, Liqi 王利器. *Yantie lun jiaozhu* 鹽鐵論校注. Beijing: Zhonghua Book Company, 1992.

Xu, Tianlin 徐天麟. *Dong Han hui yao* 東漢會要. Shanghai: Commercial Press, 1937.

Xu, Tianlin 徐天麟. *Xi Han hui yao* 西漢會要. Shanghai: Commercial Press, 1937.

Yan, Gengwang 嚴耕望. *Zhongguo difang xingzheng zhidu shi* 中國地方行政制度史, *Part I, Qin Han difang xingzheng zhidu* 秦漢地方行政制度, 2 vols. Taipei: Institute of History and Philology, 1961.

CHAPTER 3: CAO PI

Chen, Shou 陳壽. *San guo zhi* 三國志. Beijing: Zhonghua shuju, 1962.

Chen, Zhi 陳直 *Han shu xin zheng* 漢書新証. 2nd ed. Tianjin: Renmin chubanshe, 1979.

Cheng, Shude 程樹德. *Jiuchao lu kao* 九朝律考. Beijing: Zhonghua shuju, 1963.

Crespigny, Rafe De, et al. *Official Titles of the Former Han Dynasty*. Canberra: Centre of Oriental Studies in Association with Australian National University Press, 1967.

Crespigny, Rafe De. *Northern Frontier: The Policies and Strategy of the Later Han Empire*. Canberra: Faculty of Asian Studies Australian National University, 1984.

Crespigny, Rafe De, *Emperor Huan and Emperor Ling*. Canberra: Faculty of Asian Studies, The Australian National University, 1989.

Crespigny, Rafe De. *Generals of the South: The foundation and early history of The Three Kingdoms State of Wu*. Canberra: Faculty of Asian Studies, The Australian National University, 1990.

Crespigny, Richard Rafe. *A Biographical Dictionary of Later Han to the Three Kingdoms: (23–220 AD.)* Leiden: Brill, 2007.

Crespigny, Rafe De. *Imperial Warlord: A Biography of Cao Cao 155–220 AD*. Leiden: Brill, 2010.

Crespigny, Rafe De. *Fire over Luoyang: A History of the Later Han Dynasty 23–220 AD*. Leiden: Brill, 2017.

Duan, Chengshi 段成式. *Youyang Za* 酉陽雜俎. Beijing: Xueyuan Chubanshe, 2001.

Fan, Ye 范曄. *Hou Han shu* 後漢書. Beijing: Zhonghua Book Company, 1962.

Fang, Xuanling 房玄齡. *Jin shu* 晉書. Beijing: Zhonghua Book Company, 1974.

Goodman, Howard L. *Ts'ao P'i Transcendent: Political Culture and Dynasty-Founding in China at the End of the Han*. London: Routledge & CRC Press, 1998.

Goodman, Howard L. *Xun Xu and the Politics of Precision in Third-Century AD China*. Leiden: Brill, 2010.

Gu, Yanwu 顧炎武, Huang Rucheng黃如成 ed. *Rizhi lu jishi* 日知錄集釋. Changsha: Yuelu, 1994.

Kang, Youwei 康有為. *Xinxue wei jing kao* 新學偽經考. 1891, rpt. Beijing: Zhonghua Book Company, 1956.

Ku, Pan. *The History of the Former Han Dynasty* 前漢書: *a Critical Translation with Annotations by Homer H. Dubs*. Baltimore: Waverly Press, 1938.

Kuang, Ssu-ma, The Chronicle of the Three Kingdoms, Cambridge: Harvard University Press, 1962.

Lewis, Mark Edward. *The Construction of Space in Early China*. Albany: State University of New York Press, 2005.

Li, Fang李昉. *Taiping yulan* 太平御覽. Taipei: Taiwan shangwu, 1967.

Loewe, Michael. *A Biographical Dictionary of the Qin, Former Han and Xin Periods 221 BC–AD 24*. Leiden: Brill, 2000.

Loewe, Michael. *Everyday Life in Early Imperial China during the Han Period, 202 BC–220 AD*. London: Batsford, 1968.

Loewe, Michael. *The Government of the Qin and Han Empires: 221 BC–220 AD*. Hackett Pub. Co., 2006.

Loewe, Michael, and Edward L. Shaughnessy. *The Cambridge History of Ancient China: from the Origins of Civilization to 221 B.C.* Cambridge: Cambridge University Press, 2007.

Ma, Duanlin 馬端臨. *Wenxian tongkao* 文獻通考. Shanghai: Commercial Press, 1936.

Ruan, Yuan 阮元 ed. *Shisan jing zhushu* 十三經注疏. Beijing: Zhonghua Book Company, 1991.

Sawyer, Ralph D. *Sun-tzu The Art of War in Translation*. New York: Barnes & Noble, 1994.

Sima, Guang 司馬光. *Zizhi Tongjian* 資治通鑑. Shanghai: Shanghai Shudian, 1989.

Xu, Tianlin 徐天麟, *Dong Han hui yao* 東漢會要. Taibei: Shijie, 1971.

Xu, Tianlin 徐天麟, *Xi Han hui yao* 西漢會要. Taibei: Shijie, 1971.

CHAPTER 4: LI SHIMIN

Bingham, Woodbidge. *The Founding of the T'ang Dynasty: The Fall of Sui and Rise of T'ang*. Baltimore: Waverly Press, 1941.

Cen, Zhongmian 岑仲勉. *Sui Tang shi* 隋唐史. Beijing: Zhonghua shuju, 1982.

Chen, Yinke 陳寅恪. *Sui Tang Zhi Du Yuan Yuan Lve Lun Gao* 隋唐制度淵源略論稿. Taipei: The Commercial Press Taiwan, 1998.

Chen, Yinke. *Tang dai zhengzhishi shulun gao* 唐代政治史述論稿, Shijiazhuang: Hebei Jiaoyu Chubanshe, 2002.

Chiu-Duke, Josephine. "Lu Chih (754–805): Imperial Adviser and Court Official". In *Confucian Personalities, edited by* Arthur F. Wright and Denis Twitchett, 84–122. Stanford, CA: Stanford University Press, 1962.

Chiu-Duke, Josephine. *To Rebuild the Empire: Lu Chih's Confucian Pragmatist Approach to the Mid-T'ang Predicament*. Albany, NY: State University of New York Press, 2000.

Duan, Chengshi 段成式. *Youyang Zazu* 酉陽雜俎. Beijing: Xueyuan Chubanshe, 2001.

Fitzgerald, Charles Patrick. *Son of Heaven — A biography of Li Shih-Min, Founder of the T'ang Dynasty*. London: Cambridge University Press, 1933.

Gu, Yanwu 顧炎武, Huang Rucheng黃如成 ed. *Rizhi lu jishi* 日知錄集釋. Changsha: Yuelu, 1994.

Hao, Dong 董浩 ed. *Quan Tangwen* 全唐文. Beijing: Zhonghua, 1983.

Hartwell, Robert M. "Demographic, Political, and Social Transformations of China, 750–1550". *Harvard Journal of Asiatic Studies* 42, no. 2 (1982): 365–442.

Li, Fang李昉. *Taiping guangji* 太平廣記. Beijing: Zhonghua shuju, 1961.

Li, Fang李昉. *Taiping yulan* 太平御覽. Taipei: Taiwan shangwu, 1967.

Li, Jinxiu 李錦綉. *Tang dai caizhengshi gao* 唐代財政史稿. Beijing: Beijing daxue chubanshe, 2001.

Li, Zhao 李肇. *Tang guoshi bu* 唐國史補. 1957, rpt. Shanghai: Shanghai guji chubanshe, 1979.

Liu, James T.C., and Peter J. Golas eds. *Change in Sung China: Innovation or Renovation*? Lexington, Mass.: Heath, 1969.

Liu, Junwen 劉俊文. *Tang lü shuyi jianjie* 唐律疏議箋解. Beijing: Zhonghua shuju, 1996.

Liu, Xu 劉昫 et al. *Jiu Tang shu* 舊唐書. 1975, rpt. Beijing: Zhonghua shuju, 2002.

Ma, Duanlin 馬端臨. *Wenxian tongkao* 文獻通考. Shanghai: Commercial Press, 1936.

Naito, Konan 內藤湖南, *Naito Konan zenshu* 內藤湖南全集 vol. 5 (Tokyo: Chikuma shobo, 1967)

Ouyang, Xiu 歐陽修. *Xin Tang shu* 新唐書. Beijing: Zhonghua shuju, 1975.

Quan, Hansheng 全漢昇. "Tang-Song diguo yu yunhe" 唐宋帝國與運河. In *Zhongguo jingji shi yanjiu* 中國經濟史研究, 265–395. Hong Kong: Xinya yanjiusuo, 1976.

Quan, Hansheng 全漢昇, "Tang dai wujia de biandong" 唐代物價的變動. In *Guoli Zhongyang yanjiuyuan Lishi yuyan yanjiusuo jikan* 國立中央研究院 歷史語言研究所 集刊 11. 1944, rpt. Shanghai: Shangwu yinshuguan, 1947.

Ruan, Yuan 阮元 ed. *Shisan jing zhushu* 十三經注疏. Beijing: Zhonghua Book Company, 1991.

Sawyer, Ralph D. *Sun-tzu The Art of War in Translation.* New York: Barnes & noble, 1994.

Sima, Guang 司馬光. *Zizhi Tongjian* 資治通鑑. Shanghai: Shanghai Shudian, 1989.

Tao, Jingshen 陶晉生. *The Jurchen in Twelfth Century China: A Study of Sinicization.* Seattle: University of Washington Press, 1976.

Tonami, Mamoru 礪波護. *Studies in the Political and Social History of Tang China.* Kyoto: DOHOSHA Printing, 1986.

Twitchett, Denis C. ed. *The Cambridge History of China, Vol. 3: Sui and T'ang China, 589–906, Part 1.* 1979, rpt. New York: Cambridge University Press, 2007.

Twitchett, Denis C. *Financial Administration under the T'ang Dynasty.* Cambridge: Cambridge University Press, 1971.

Twitchett, Denis C. *The Writing of Official History under the Tang.* Cambridge: Cambridge University Press, 1992.

Wang, Pu 王溥. *Tang huiyao* 唐會要. Beijing: Zhonghua shuju, 1955.

Wang, Qinruo 王欽若 et al., *Cefu yuangui* 冊府元龜. Beijing: Zhonghua, 1960.

Wechsler, Howard J. *Mirror to the Son of Heaven — Wei Cheng at the Court of T'ang T'ai-tsung.* New Haven: Yale University Press, 1974.

Wen, Daya 溫大雅. *Da Tang chuangye qiju zhu* 大唐創業起居注. Shanghai: Shanghai Guji Chubanshe [Shanghai Chinese Classics Publishing House], 1983.

Wright, Arthur F., and Denis Twitchett, eds. *Perspectives on the T'ang.* New Haven, CT: Yale University Press, 1973.

Wright Arthur F. *The Sui Dynasty: The Unification of China, A.D. 581–617.* New York: Knoopf, 1978.

Wu, Jing 吳. *Zhenguan zhenyao* 貞觀政要. Shanghai: Shanghai guji chubanshe, 1978.

Zhangsun, Wuji 長孫無忌. *Tanglu shuyi* 唐律疏義. Beijing: Zhonghua shuju, 1983.

Zheng, Wei 魏徵 ed. *Sui shu* 隋書. Beijing: Zhonghua Book Company, 1973.

CHAPTER 5: LI ZHI

Abramson, Marc S. *Ethnic Identity in Tang China*. Philadelphia: University of Pennsylvania Press, 2007.

Allen, Sarah M. *Shifting Stories: History, Gossip and Love in Narrative from Tang Dynasty China*. Cambridge: Harvard University Asia Center, 2014.

Cawthorne, Nigel. *Daughter of heaven: the true story of the only woman to become Emperor of China*. England: One World Publications, 2007.

Chen, Yinke. *Tang dai zhengzhishi shulun gao* 唐代政治史述論稿. Shijiazhuang: Hebei jiaoyu chubanshe, 2002.

Chen, Yinke 陳寅恪. "Wu Zhao yu fojiao" 武曌與佛教. In *Jinmingguan conggao erbian* 金明館叢稿二編 edited by Chen Yinke, 137–155. Shanghai: Shanghai Guji Chubanshe, 1980.

Clements, Jonathan. *Wu: The Chinese Empress Who Schemed, Seduced and Murdered Her Way to Become a Living God*. Stroud: Sutton, 2007.

Davis, Richard L. *Fire and Ice: Li Cunxu and the Founding of the Later Tang*. Aberdeen: Hong Kong University Press, 2016

Duan, Chengshi 段成式. *Youyang Zazu* 酉陽雜俎. Beijing: Xueyuan Chubanshe, 2001.

Fairbank, John K., and Edwin O. Reischauer. "The Late T'ang and Sung: The Flowering of Chinese Culture." In *China: Traditional and Transformation*. Rev. ed. 116–151. Boston: Houghton Mifflin Co., 1989.

Fitzgerald, Charles Patrick. *The Empress Wu*. London: Cresset Press, 1968.

Goldin, Paul Rakita. *The Culture of Sex in Ancient China*. Honolulu: University of Hawai'I Press, 2002.

Guisso, R.W.L., and Standley Johannesen ed. *Women in China*. Amsterdam: Philo Press, 1978.

Guisso, R.W.L. *Wu Tse-T'ien and the Politics of Legitimation in T'ang China* Bellingham: Western Washington University Press, 2002.

Hao, Dong 董浩 ed. *Quan Tangwen* 全唐文. Beijing: Zhonghua, 1983.

Li, Fang 李昉. *Taiping guangji* 太平廣記. Beijing: Zhonghua shuju, 1961.

Li, Fang 李昉. *Taiping yulan* 太平御覽. Taipei: Taiwan shangwu, 1967.

Liu, Junwen 劉俊文. *Tang lü shuyi jianjie* 唐律疏議箋解. Beijing: Zhonghua shuju, 1996.

Liu, Xu 劉昫 et al., *Jiu Tang shu* 舊唐書. 1975, rpt. Beijing: Zhonghua shuju, 2002.

Ma, Duanlin 馬端臨. *Wenxian tongkao* 文獻通考. Shanghai: Commercial Press, 1936.

Millan, Betty. *Monstrous Regiment: Women Rulers in Men's Worlds*. Windsor: Kensal Press, 1982.

Naito, Konan 內藤湖南. *Naito Konan zenshu* 內藤湖南全集 vol. 5. Tokyo: Chikuma shobo, 1967.

Ouyang, Xiu 歐陽修. *Xin Tang shu* 新唐書. Beijing: Zhonghua shuju, 1975.

Peterson, C.A. "Court and Province in Mid and Late- T'ang". In *The Cambridge History of China vol. 3: Sui and T'ang China*, edited by Denis C. Twitchett, 589–906. Cambridge: Cambridge University Press, 1979.

Rothschild, N. Harry. *Wu Zhao: China's only woman emperor*. London: Pearson Longman, 2008.

Rouzer, Paul F. *Articulated Ladies: Gender and the Male Community in Early Chinese Texts*. Cambridge: Harvard University Asia Center, 2001.

Ruan, Fangfu 阮芳賦. *Sex in China — Studies in Sexology in Chinese Culture*. New York: Plenum Press, 1991.

Ruan, Yuan 阮元 ed. *Shisan jing zhushu* 十三經注疏. Beijing: Zhonghua Book Company, 1991.

Schafer, Edward H. *The Divine Women: Dragon Ladies and Rain Maides in T'ang Literature*. Berkeley: University of California, 1973.

Sima, Guang 司馬光. *Zizhi Tongjian* 資治通鑑. Shanghai: Shanghai Shudian, 1989.

Tonami, Mamoru 礪波護. *Studies in the Political and Social History of Tang China*. Kyoto: DOHOSHA Printing, 1986.

Wang, Pu 王溥. *Tang huiyao* 唐會要. Beijing: Zhonghua shuju, 1955.

Wang, Qinruo 王欽若 et al. *Cefu yuangui* 冊府元龜. Beijing: Zhonghua Book Company, 1960.

Zhangsun, Wuji 長孫無忌. *Tanglu shuyi* 唐律疏義. Beijing: Zhonghua shuju, 1983.

CHAPTER 6: LI LONGJI

Abramson, Marc S. *Ethnic Identity in Tang China*. Philadelphia: University of Pennsylvania Press, 2007.

Allen, Sarah M. *Shifting Stories: History, Gossip and Love in Narrative from Tang Dynasty China*. Cambridge: Harvard University Asia Center, 2014.

Cawthorne, Nigel. *Daughter of heaven: the true story of the only woman to become Emperor of China*. England: One World Publications, 2007.

Chen, Yinke. *Tang dai zhengzhishi shulun gao* 唐代政治史述論稿. Shijiazhuang: Hebei jiaoyu chubanshe, 2002.

Clements, Jonathan. *Wu: The Chinese Empress Who Schemed, Seduced and Murdered Her Way to Become a Living God*. Stroud: Sutton, 2007.

Davis, Richard L. *Fire and Ice: Li Cunxu and the Founding of the Later Tang*. Aberdeen: Hong Kong University Press, 2016.

Du, You 杜佑. *Tongdian* 通典. Beijing: Zhonghua shuju, 1988.

Duan, Chengshi 段成式. *Youyang Zazu* 酉陽雜俎. Beijing: Xueyuan Chubanshe, 2001.

Hao, Dong 董浩 ed. *Quan Tangwen* 全唐文. Beijing: Zhonghua, 1983.

Lewis, Edward Mark. *China's Cosmopolitan Empire: The Tang Dynasty*. Cambridge: Harvard University Press, 2009.

Li, Fang 李昉. *Taiping guangji* 太平廣記. Beijing: Zhonghua shuju, 1961.

Li, Fang 李昉. *Taiping yulan* 太平御覽. Taipei: Taiwan shangwu, 1967.

Liu, Junwen 劉俊文. *Tang lü shuyi jianjie* 唐律疏議箋解. Beijing: Zhonghua shuju, 1996.

Liu, Xu 劉昫 et al. *Jiu Tang shu* 舊唐書. 1975, rpt. Beijing: Zhonghua shuju, 2002.

Liu, Zhiji 劉知幾. *Shitong* 史通. Shanghai: Shanghai guji, 2008.

Ma, Duanlin 馬端臨. *Wenxian tongkao* 文獻通考. Shanghai: Commercial Press, 1936.

Millan, Betty. *Monstrous Regiment: Women Rulers in Men's Worlds*. Windsor: Kensal Press, 1982.

Naito, Konan 內藤湖南. *Naito Konan zenshu* 內藤湖南全集 vol.5. Tokyo: Chikuma shobo, 1967.

Ouyang, Xiu 歐陽修. *Xin Tang shu* 新唐書. Beijing: Zhonghua shuju, 1975.

Ouyang, Xun 歐陽詢, Linghu Defe令狐德芬, Yuan Lang 袁朗, and Zhao Hongzhi趙宏智.*Yiwen leiju*藝文類聚. Shanghai: Shanghai Guji Chubanshe, 1999.

Peterson, C.A. "Court and Province in Mid and Late- T'ang". In *The Cambridge History of China vol. 3: Sui and T'ang China*, edited by Denis C. Twitchett, 589–906. Cambridge: Cambridge University Press, 1979.

Pulleyblank, Edwin G. *The Background of the Rebellion of An Lu-shan*. London: Oxford University Press, 1982.

Ruan, Yuan 阮元 ed. *Shisan jing zhushu* 十三經注疏. Beijing: Zhonghua Book Company, 1991.

Sima, Guang 司馬光. *Zizhi Tongjian* 資治通鑑. Shanghai: Shanghai Shudian, 1989.

Tonami, Mamoru 礪波護. *Studies in the Political and Social History of Tang China*. Kyoto: DOHOSHA Printing, 1986.

Twitchett, Denis. *Financial Administration under the Tang Dynasty*. Cambridge: Cambridge University Press, 1970.

Twitchett, Denis. *The Writing of Official History under the Tang*. Cambridge: Cambridge University Press, 1992.

Wang, Jing 王淫. *Da-Tang kaiyuan li* 大唐開元禮. Beijing: Min zu chu ban she 民族出版社, 2000.

Wang, Pu 王溥. *Tang huiyao* 唐會要. Beijing: Zhonghua shuju, 1955.

Wang, Qinruo 王欽若 et al. *Cefu yuangui* 冊府元龜. Beijing: Zhonghua Book Company, 1960.

Wang, Shounan 王壽南. *Tangdai fanzhen yu zhongyang guanxi zhi yanjiu* 唐代藩鎮與中央關係之研究. Taiwan: Guoli zhengzhi daxue zhengzhi yanjiu-suo, 1969.

Wang, Yinglin 王應麟. *Yu hai* 玉海. Yangzhou: Guangling shushe, 2007.

Wu, Tingxie 吳廷燮. *Tang fangzhen nianbiao* 唐方鎮年表. Beijing: Zhonghua shuju, 1980.

Zhang, Guogang 張國剛. *Tangdai fanzhen yanjiu* 唐代藩鎮研究. Changsha: Hunan jiaoyu chubanshe, 1987.

Zhang, Qun章群. *Tangdai fanjiang yanjiu* 唐代蕃將研究. Taipei: Lianjing, 1986.

Zhangsun, Wuji長孫無忌. *Tanglu shuyi* 唐律疏義. Beijing: Zhonghua shuju, 1983.

CHAPTER 7: HONG TAIJI

A, gui 阿桂. *Man zhou yuan liu kao* 满洲源流考. Shen yang: Liao ning min zu chu ban she, 1988.

Bruzzi, Stella. *New Qing Imperial History: The Making of Inner Asian Empire at Qing*. Abingdon: Routledge, 2011.

Chang, Michael G. *A Court on Horseback: Imperial Touring and the Construction of Qing Rule, 1680–1785*. Cambridge: Harvard University Asia Center, 2007.

Chen, Jiahua 陳佳華. "Baqi zhidu 八旗制度". In *Zhongguo da baike quanshu* 中國大百科全書. Beijing/Shanghai: Zhongguo da baike quanshu chu-banshe, 1992.

E'ertai 鄂爾泰. *Ba qi tong zhi chu ji*八旗通志初集. Taipei: Tai wan xue sheng shu ju 臺灣學生書局, 1968.

E'ertai 鄂爾泰, Zhang Tingyu 張廷玉. *Qing Taizu Nu'erhachi shi lu* 清太祖努爾哈赤實錄. Shanghai: Shanghai shu dian, 1989.

Elliott, Mark C. "Ethnicity in the Qing Eight Banners". In *Empire at the Margins: Culture, Ethnicity, and Frontier in Early Modern China*, edited by Pamela

Kyle Crossley, Helen F. Siu, and Donald S. Sutton. Berkeley: University of California Press, 2006.

Elliott, Mark C. *The Manchu Way the Eight Banners and Ethnic Identity in Late Imperial China*. California: Stanford University Press, 2009.

Franz, Michael. *The Origin of Manchu Rule in China: Frontier and Bureaucracy as Interacting Force in the Chinese Empire*. Baltimore: John Hopkins University Press, 1942.

He, Changling 賀長齡. *Huang chao jing shi wen bian* 皇朝經世文編. Taipei: Wen hai chu ban she, 1972.

He, Changling 賀長齡. *Huang chao jing shi wen bian xu bian* 皇朝經世文續編. Taipei: Wen hai chu ban she, 1972.

Hostetler, Laura. *Qing Colonial Enterprise: Ethnography and Cartography in Early Modern China*. Chicago: University of Chicago Press, 2005.

Huang, Zhangjian 黃彰健. *Ming shi lu* 明實錄. Nangang: Zhong yang yan jiu yuan li shi yu yan yan jiu suo, 1962–1968.

Huang, Zongxi 黃宗羲. *Ming yi dai fang lu* 明夷待訪錄. Taipei: Tai wan shang wu, 1965.

Ji, Huang 嵇璜. *Qin ding Xu Tong Dian* 欽定續通典. Shanghai: Shanghai gu ji chu ban she, 1987.

Ji, Huang 嵇璜. *Qin ding Xu Wen Xian Tong kao* 欽定續文獻通考. Shanghai: Hong bao shu ju, 1902.

Ko, Dorothy. *Teachers of the inner Chambers: Women and Culture in Seventeenth Century China*. Sandford: Stanford University Press, 1994.

Kuhn, Philip. *Rebellion and Its Enemies in Late Imperial China; Militarization and Social Structure 1796–1864*. Cambridge: Harvard University Press, 1970.

Kuhn, Philip. *Soulstealers: The Chinese Sorcery Scare of 1768*. Cambridge: Harvard University Press, 1990

Kun'gang 崑岡. *Qing hui dian* 清會典. Beijing: Zhonghua shu ju, 1991.

Liaoning sheng dang an guan 遼寧市檔案館. *Qing sheng xun* 清聖訓. Beijing: Zhongguo dang an chu ban she, 2010.

Mai, Zhonghua 麥仲華. *Huang chao jing shi wen xin bian* 皇朝經世文新編. Taipei: Wen hai chu ban she, 1972.

Mann, Susan. *Precious Records: Women in China's Long Eighteenth Century*. Stanford: Stanford University Press, 1997.

Min, Tu-ki, and Philip A. Kuhn ed. *National Polity and Local Power: The Transformation of Late Imperial China*. Cambridge: Harvard University Asia Center, 1990.

Nan, Bing Wen 南炳文. *Jiao zheng tai chang tian qi qi ju zhu* 校正泰昌天啓起居注. Tian Jin: Tian jin gu ji chu ban she, 2012.

Perdue, Peter C. *China Marches West: The Qing Conquest of Central Eurasia*. Cambridge: Harvard University Press, 2005.

Qi, Meiqin 祁美琴. *Qingdai neiwufu* 清代內務府. Beijing: Zhongguo renmin daxue chubanshe, 1998.

Rawski, Evelyn S. *The Last Emperors: A Social History of Qing Imperial Institutions*. Berkeley: University of California Press, 2001.

Ruan, Yuan 阮元 ed. *Shisan jing zhushu* 十三經注疏. Beijing: Zhonghua, 1991.

Sawyer, Ralph D. *Sun-tzu The Art of War in Translation*. New York: Barnes & Noble, 1994.

Shi, Zhihong 史志宏. "Manzhou shilu 滿洲實錄". In *Zhongguo da baike quanshu* 中國大百科全書. Beijing/Shanghai: Zhongguo da baike quanshu chubanshe, 1992.

Spence, Jonathan D. *Return to Dragon Mountain: Memories of a Late Ming Man*. New York: Viking Books, 2007.

Tao, Jingshen 陶晉生. *Nuzhen shilun* 女真史論. Taipei: Shihuo, 1981.

Twitchett, Denis, and John K. Fairbank. *Cambridge History of China: Volume 9, The Ch`ing Empire to 1800*. Cambridge: Cambridge University Press, 2002.

Wakeman, Frederic. *The Great Enterprise Volume 1: The Manchu Reconstruction of Imperial Order in Seventeenth Century China*. California: University of California Press, 1986.

Wang, Shan 王琰. *Wan shou sheng dian chu ji* 萬壽盛典初集. Shanghai: Shanghai gu ji chu ban she, 1987.

Wang, Xianqian 王先謙. *Shi yi chao dong hua lu* 十一朝東華錄. Beijing: Yan shi chu ban she, 1999.

Xu, Ke 徐珂. *Qing bai lei chao* 清稗類鈔. Beijing: Zhonghua shu ju, 2010.

Xu, Pu 徐溥. *Ming hui dian* 明會典. Shanghai: Shanghai gu ji chu ban she, 1987.

Zhao, er xun 趙爾巽. *Qing shi gao* 清史稿. Tian jin: Tian jin gu ji chu ban she, 2012.

CHAPTER 8: YINZHEN

Chang, Chung-li. *The Chinese Gentry: Studies on Their Role in Nineteenth Century Chinese Society*. Seattle: University of Washington Press, 1955.

Elliott, Mark C. *Emperor Qianlong: Son of Heaven, Man of the World*. London: Pearson Longman, 2009.

Freedman, Maurice. *Lineage Organization in Southeastern China*. London: Athlone, 1958.

He, Changling 賀長齡. *Huang chao jing shi wen bian* 皇朝經世文編. Taipei: Wen hai chu ban she, 1972.

He, Changling 賀長齡. *Huang chao jing shi wen bian xu bian* 皇朝經世文續編. Taibei: Wen hai chu ban she, 1972.

Ji, Huang 嵇璜. *Qin ding Xu Tong Dian* 欽定續通典. Shanghai: Shanghai gu ji chu ban she, 1987.

Ji, Huang 嵇璜. *Qin ding Xu Wen Xian Tong kao* 欽定續文獻通考. Shanghai: Hong bao shu ju, 1902.

Kun'gang 崑岡. *Qing hui dian* 清會典. Beijing: Zhonghua shuju, 1991.

Li, Xu 李煦. *Li Xu zouzhe* 李煦奏折. Beijing: Zhonghua shuju, 1976.

Liaoning sheng dang an guan 遼寧市檔案館. *Qing sheng xun* 清聖訓. Beijing: Zhongguo dang an chu ban she, 2010.

Mai, Zhonghua 麥仲華. *Huang chao jing shi wen xin bian* 皇朝經世文新編. Taipei: Wen hai chu ban she,1972.

Qi, Meiqin 祁美琴. *Qingdai neiwufu* 清代內務府. Beijing: Zhongguo renmin daxue chubanshe, 1998.

Ruan, Yuan 阮元 ed. *Shisan jing zhushu* 十三經注疏. Beijing: Zhonghua, 1991.

Sawyer, Ralph D. *Sun-tzu The Art of War in Translation*. New York: Barnes & noble, 1994.

Spence, Jonathan D. *Emperor of China: Self-Portrait of K'ang-hsi*. New York: Vintage Books, 1988.

Spence, Jonathan D. *Treason by the Book*. London: Penguin Books, 2001.

Spence, Jonathan D. *Ts'ao Yin and the K'ang-hsi Emperor: Bondservant and Master*. London: Yale University Press, 2009.

Teng, Ssu-yu, and John K. Fairbank. *China's Response to the West. A Documentary Survey 1839–1923*. Cambridge: Harvard University Press, 1954.

Twitchett, Denis, and John K. Fairbank. *Cambridge History of China: Volume 9, The Ch`ing Empire to 1800*. Cambridge: Cambridge University Press, 2002.

Wang, Shan 王琰. *Wan shou sheng dian chu ji* 萬壽盛典初集. Shanghai: Shanghai gu ji chu ban she, 1987.

Wang, Xianqian 王先謙. *Shi yi chao dong hua lu* 十一朝東華錄. Beijing: Yan shi chu ban she, 1999.

Wu, Silas. *Communication and Imperial Control in China: Evolution of the Palace Memorial System* 1693–1735. Cambridge: Harvard University Press, 1970.

Xu, Ke 徐珂. *Qing bai lei chao* 清稗類鈔. Beijing: Zhonghua shu ju, 2010.

Zhao, er xun 趙爾巽. *Qing shi gao* 清史稿. Tianjin: Tian jin gu ji chu ban she, 2012.

Zhongguo di 1 li shi dang an guan 中國第一歷史檔案館 ed. *Qing dai qi ju zhu ce Yongzheng chao* 清代起居注冊雍正朝. Beijing: Zhonghua shu ju, 2016.

Zhuang, Jufa 莊吉發. *Qing dai zou zhe zhi du* 清代奏摺制度. Taipei: Guo li guorto bo wu yuan, 1979.

Zou, Ailian 鄒愛蓮 ed. *Qing dai qi ju zhu ce Kangxi chao* 清代起居注冊康熙朝. Beijing: Zhonghua shu ju, 2009.

CHAPTER 9: YIZHU

Arlington, Lewis Charles. *Through the Dragon's Eyes. Fifty Years' Experience of a Foreigner in the Chinese Government Service*. London: Constable and Co. Ltd., 1931.

Bland, J.O.P., and E. Backhouse. *China under the Empress Dowager, Being the History of the Life and Times of Tzui-his*. London: William Heinemann, 1911.

Chang, Chung-li. *The Chinese Gentry: Studies on Their Role in Nineteenth Century Chinese Society*. Seattle: University of Washington Press, 1955.

Ch'en, Jerome, and Yuan Shih-k'ai. *Brutus Assumes the Purple*. Stanford: Stanford University Press, 1961.

Chiang, Siang-tseh. *The Nien Rebellion*. Seattle: University of Washington Press, 1954.

Ch'u, T'ung-tsu. *Local Government in China Under the Ch'ing*. Cambridge: Harvand University Press, 1962.

Feuerwerker, Albert. *China's Early Industrialization: Sheng Hsuan-huai 1844–1916 and Mandarin Enterprise*. Cambridge: Harvard University Press, 1958.

Gui, Qingyang 桂清楊. *Qing dai qi ju zhu ce tong zhi zhao* 清代起居注冊同治朝. Taipei: Lian jing fa xing, 1983.

He, Changling 賀長齡. *Huang chao jing shi wen bian* 皇朝經世文編. Taipei: Wen hai chu ban she, 1972.

He, Changling 賀長齡. *Huang chao jing shi wen bian xu bian* 皇朝經世文續編. Taipei: Wen hai chu ban she, 1972.

Kuhn, Philip. *Rebellion and Its Enemies in Late Imperial China*. Cambridge: Harvard University Press, 1970.

Kun'gang 崑岡. *Qing hui dian* 清會典. Beijing: Zhonghua shu ju, 1991.

Liaoning sheng dang an guan 遼寧市檔案館. *Qing sheng xun* 清聖訓. Beijing: Zhongguo dang an chu ban she, 2010.

Mai, Zhonghua 麥仲華. *Huang chao jing shi wen xin bian* 皇朝經世文新編. Taipei: Wen hai chu ban she, 1972.

Princess Der Ling. *Son of Heaven: A Life of the Emperor Kuang Hsu*. New York: Appleton-Century, 1935.

Qi, Meiqin 祁美琴. *Qingdai neiwufu* 清代內務府. Beijing: Zhongguo renmin daxue chubanshe, 1998.

Ruan, Yuan 阮元 ed. *Shisan jing zhushu* 十三經注疏. Beijing: Zhonghua, 1991.

Sawyer, Ralph D. *Sun-tzu The Art of War in Translation*. New York: Barnes & Noble, 1994.

Shen, Zhaolin 沈兆霖. *Qing dai qi ju zhu ce Xianfeng chao* 清代起居注冊咸豐朝. Taipei: Lian jing fa xing, 1983.

Spence, Jonathan D. *God's Chinese Son: The Taiping Heavenly Kingdom of Hong Xiuquan*. New York: W.W. Norton & company, 1996.

Spence, Jonathan D. *To Change China: Western Advisers in China*. London: Penguin Books, 2002.

Teng, Ssu-yu, and John K. Fairbank. *China's Response to the West. A Documentary Survey 1839–1923*. Cambridge: Harvard University Press, 1954.

Wakeman Jr., Frederic. *Fall of Imperial China*. New York: The Free Press, 1975.

Wakeman Jr., Frederic. *Strangers at the Gate: Social Disorder in South China, 1839–1861*. California: University of California Press, 1997.

Wang, Xianqian 王先謙. *Shi yi chao dong hua lu* 十一朝東華錄. Beijing: Yan shi chu ban she, 1999.

Watson, James L. *Death Ritual in Late Imperial and Modern China*. California: University of California Press, 1988.

Wright, Mary Clabaugh. *The Last Stand of Chinese Conservatism. The T'ung-Chih Restoration 1862–1874*. Stanford: Stanford University Press, 1957.

Wright, Stanley F. *Hart and the Chinese Customs*. Belfast: Wm. Mullan and Son, Ltd., 1950.

Xu, Ke 徐珂. *Qing bai lei chao* 清稗類鈔. Beijing: Zhonghua shu ju, 2010.

Xu, Zhixiang 徐致祥. *Qing dai qi ju zhu ce Guang xu zhao* 清代起居注冊光緒朝. Taipei: Lian jing, 1987.

Yi, Yuanshan 易元善. *Qing dai qi ju zhu ce Dao guang zhao* 清代起居注冊道光朝. Taipei: Lian jing fa xing, 1985.

Zhao, Er Xun 趙爾巽. *Qing shi gao* 清史稿. Tian jin: Tian jin gu ji chu ban she, 2012.

APPENDIX 1: OVERVIEW OF THE SUCCESSION PROCESS IN ANCIENT CHINA

Ban, Gu 班固. *Han shu* 漢書. Beijing: Zhonghua, 1962.

Cen, Zhongmian 岑仲勉. *Sui Tang shi* 隋唐史. Beijing: Zhonghua shuju, 1982.

Fang, Xuanling 房玄齡. *Jin shu* 晉書. Beijing: Zhonghua, 1974.

Huang, Zhangjian 黃彰健. *Ming shi lu* 明實錄. Nangang: Zhong yang yan jiu yuan li shi yu yan yan jiu suo, 1962–1968.

Liu, Xiang 劉向. *Zhanguo ce* 戰國策. Shanghai: Shanghai guji, 1995.

Liu, Xu 劉昫 et al. *Jiu Tang shu* 舊唐書. 1975, rpt. Beijing: Zhonghua shuju, 2002.

Ma, Duanlin 馬端臨. *Wenxian tongkao* 文獻通考. Shanghai: Commercial Press, 1936.

Ouyang, Xiu 歐陽修. *Xin Tang shu* 新唐書. Beijing: Zhonghua shuju, 1975.

Qi, Meiqin 祁美琴. *Qingdai neiwufu* 清代內務府. Beijing: Zhongguo renmin daxue chubanshe, 1998.

Ruan, Yuan 阮元 ed. *Shisan jing zhushu* 十三經注疏. Beijing: Zhonghua, 1991.

Sima, Guang 司馬光. *Zizhi Tongjian* 資治通鑑. Shanghai: Shanghai Shudian, 1989.

Sima, Qian 司馬遷. Shi ji 史記. Beijing: Zhonghua, 1963.

Toqto'a 脫脫, *Song Shi* 宋史. Beijing: Zhonghua shuju, 1985.

Wang, Xianqian 王先謙. *Shi yi chao dong hua lu* 十一朝東華錄. Beijing: Yan shi chu ban she, 1999.

Xu, Mengshen 徐梦莘. *San chao bei meng hui bian* 三朝北盟會編. Shanghai: Shanghai guji, 2019.

Zhang, Jinguang 張金光. *Qin zhi yanjiu* 秦制研究. Shanghai: Shanghai guji, 2004.

Index